FOREIGN POLICY OF THE UNITED STATES

UNITED STATES ASSISTANCE FOR THE PALESTINIANS

Foreign Policy of the United States

Additional books in this series can be found on Nova's website under the Series tab.

Additional E-books in this series can be found on Nova's website under the E-book tab.

Global Political Studies

Additional books in this series can be found on Nova's website under the Series tab.

Additional E-books in this series can be found on Nova's website under the E-book tab.

FOREIGN POLICY OF THE UNITED STATES

UNITED STATES ASSISTANCE FOR THE PALESTINIANS

JAMES M. BAILEY
AND
PAUL F. MILLER
EDITORS

Nova Science Publishers, Inc.
New York

For permission to use material from this book please contact us:
Telephone 631-231-7269; Fax 631-231-8175
Web Site: http://www.novapublishers.com

NOTICE TO THE READER

Additional color graphics may be available in the e-book version of this book.

LIBRARY OF CONGRESS CATALOGING-IN-PUBLICATION DATA

U.S. assistance for the Palestinians / editors, James M. Bailey and Paul F. Miller.
p. cm.
Includes index.
ISBN 978-1-62100-830-9 (hardcover)
1. Economic assistance, American--Palestine. I. Bailey, James M. II. Miller, Paul F.
HC415.25.P86U83 2011
338.91'73056953--dc23
2011039660

Published by Nova Science Publishers, Inc. † New York

CONTENTS

PREFACE

U.S. aid to the Palestinians is intended to forward at least three major U.S. policy priorities of interest to Congress: 1) combating, neutralizing, and preventing terrorism against Israel from the Islamist group Hamas and other militant organizations; 2) creating a virtuous cycle of stability and prosperity in the West Bank that inclines Palestinians, including those in the Hamas-controlled Gaza Strip, towards peaceful coexistence with Israel and prepares them for self-governance; and 3) meeting humanitarian needs and preventing further destabilization, particularly in the Gaza Strip. This book examines U.S. foreign aid to the Palestinians wherein because of congressional concerns that U.S. funds might be diverted to Palestinian terrorist groups, this aid is subject to a host of vetting and oversight requirements and legislative restrictions.

Chapter 1 - Since the establishment of limited Palestinian self-rule in the West Bank and Gaza Strip in the mid-1990s, the U.S. government has committed over $4 billion in bilateral assistance to the Palestinians, who are among the world's largest per capita recipients of international foreign aid. Successive Administrations have requested aid for the Palestinians to support at least three major U.S. policy priorities of interest to Congress:

Combating, neutralizing, and preventing terrorism against Israel from the Islamist group Hamas and other militant organizations.

Creating a virtuous cycle of stability and prosperity in the West Bank that inclines Palestinians—including those in the Hamas-controlled Gaza Strip—towards peaceful coexistence with Israel and prepares them for self-governance.

Meeting humanitarian needs and preventing further destabilization, particularly in the Gaza Strip.

Chapter 2 - The 2003 Roadmap for Peace process sponsored by the United States and other nations obligates the Palestinian Authority (PA) and the Government of Israel to undertake security efforts as a necessary precursor for achieving the long-standing objective of establishing a Palestinian state as part of the two-state solution for peace in the Middle East. In 2005 the Department of State (State) created the office of the United States Security Coordinator (USSC) to help the parties meet these obligations.

GAO was asked to (1) describe the nature and extent of U.S. security assistance to the PA since 2007; (2) assess State's efforts to measure the effectiveness of its security assistance; and (3) describe factors that may affect the implementation of U.S. security assistance programs. GAO analyzed documents; interviewed officials and regional experts; and conducted fieldwork in Jerusalem, the West Bank, Israel, and Jordan.

Chapter 3 - Of the approximately $1.17 billion in ESF assistance provided by the United States to the West Bank and Gaza from fiscal years 2008 and 2009 ESF appropriations, USAID obligated a total of about $1.16 billion and expended $678.5 million, as of December 31, 2009. More specifically, as of this date, USAID obligated 100 percent and expended over 80 percent of fiscal year 2008 ESF funds for the West Bank and Gaza.[8] For fiscal year 2009, USAID obligated approximately 98 percent and expended 47 percent of the ESF funds, as of December 31, 2009. The USAID mission in Tel Aviv reported that it plans to obligate the remaining $8.3 million in fiscal year 2009 ESF funds prior to the end of fiscal year 2010. The total of $1.17 billion in ESF funds for fiscal years 2008 and 2009 represented a large increase from previous years' appropriations, which totaled $448.7 million from fiscal years 2004 through 2007.

Chapter 4 - The U.S. government is one of the largest donors to Palestinians. It provided nearly $575 million in assistance in fiscal year 2008. This assistance is provided through the U.S. Agency for International Development (USAID) and through contributions to international organizations, primarily the United Nations Relief and Works Agency for Palestine Refugees in the Near East (UNRWA). The Department of State (State) oversees U.S. contributions to UNRWA. To help ensure that U.S. funds for these programs are not provided to individuals or entities engaged in terrorist activities, USAID and State must comply with restrictions under U.S. law. GAO was asked to (1) assess the extent to which USAID has complied with its antiterrorism policies and procedures and (2) assess State's and UNRWA's policies and procedures to support conformance with U.S. statutory conditions. GAO reviewed U.S. and UNRWA documents;

interviewed USAID, State, and UNRWA officials; and conducted fieldwork in Israel, Jerusalem, and Jordan.

In: United States Assistance for the Palestinians ISBN: 978-1-62100-830-9
Editors: J. M. Bailey and P. F. Miller

Chapter 1

UNITED STATES FOREIGN AID TO THE PALESTINIANS*

Jim Zanotti

SUMMARY

Since the establishment of limited Palestinian self-rule in the West Bank and Gaza Strip in the mid-1990s, the U.S. government has committed over $4 billion in bilateral assistance to the Palestinians, who are among the world's largest per capita recipients of international foreign aid. Successive Administrations have requested aid for the Palestinians to support at least three major U.S. policy priorities of interest to Congress:

- Combating, neutralizing, and preventing terrorism against Israel from the Islamist group Hamas and other militant organizations.
- Creating a virtuous cycle of stability and prosperity in the West Bank that inclines Palestinians—including those in the Hamas-controlled Gaza Strip— towards peaceful coexistence with Israel and prepares them for self-governance.
- Meeting humanitarian needs and preventing further destabilization, particularly in the Gaza Strip.

---

* This is an edited, reformatted and augmented version of a Congressional Research Service publication, CRS Report for Congress, RS22967, from www.crs.gov, dated May 31, 2011.

Since June 2007, these U.S. policy priorities have crystallized around the factional and geographical split between the Fatah-led Palestinian Authority (PA) in the West Bank and Hamas in the Gaza Strip. A May 2011 power-sharing agreement between Fatah and Hamas has raised concerns among some Members of Congress about continuing U.S. budgetary and security assistance to a PA government that could be subject to the approval of a U.S.-designated Foreign Terrorist Organization (Hamas) that claims to reserve the right to violently oppose Israel's existence. Prospects for implementation of the power-sharing agreement remain unclear. Some observers question the extent to which Palestinians in the West Bank and Gaza are likely to integrate their political decisionmaking and security practices, and also question the credibility of the one-year timeline put forward for PA presidential and legislative elections. Furthermore, some U.S. lawmakers have raised the possibility that U.S. aid to the PA could be affected by Palestinian efforts to seek international recognition of Palestinian statehood outside of negotiations with Israel.

From FY2008 to the present, annual U.S. bilateral assistance to the West Bank and Gaza Strip has averaged over $600 million, including annual averages of over $200 million in direct budgetary assistance and over $100 million in non-lethal security assistance for the PA in the West Bank. Additionally, the United States is the largest single-state donor to the U.N. Relief and Works Agency for Palestine Refugees in the Near East (UNRWA). However, whether UNRWA's role is beneficial remains a polarizing question, particularly with respect to its presence in Hamas-controlled Gaza.

Because of congressional concerns that, among other things, funds might be diverted to Palestinian terrorist groups, U.S. aid is subject to a host of vetting and oversight requirements and legislative restrictions. U.S. assistance to the Palestinians is given alongside assistance from other international donors, and U.S. policymakers routinely call for greater or more timely assistance from Arab governments in line with their pledges.

The power-sharing or "unity" government expected in the wake of the May 2011 Fatah-Hamas agreement will not be eligible for U.S. aid if Hamas is included in the government and does not change its stance towards Israel—possibly subject to some limited exceptions. Even if the immediate objectives of U.S. assistance programs for the Palestinians are met, lack of progress toward a politically legitimate and peaceful two-state solution could undermine the utility of U.S. aid in helping the Palestinians become more cohesive, stable, and self-reliant over the long term.

INTRODUCTION: ISSUES FOR CONGRESS

U.S. aid to the Palestinians is intended to forward at least three major U.S. policy priorities of interest to Congress:

- Combating, neutralizing, and preventing terrorism against Israel from the Islamist group Hamas and other militant organizations.
- Creating a virtuous cycle of stability and prosperity in the West Bank that inclines Palestinians—including those in the Hamas-controlled Gaza Strip— towards peaceful coexistence with Israel and prepares them for self-governance.
- Meeting humanitarian needs and preventing further destabilization, particularly in the Gaza Strip.

Since June 2007, these U.S. policy priorities have crystallized around the geographical and factional split between

1) *West Bank/Fatah*: the U.S.- and Western-supported Palestinian Authority (PA) in the West Bank led by President Mahmoud Abbas (who also leads the secular nationalist Fatah faction) and Prime Minister Salam Fayyad (a political independent and former international technocrat); and
2) *Gaza Strip/Hamas*: the regime led by Hamas in Gaza, which receives support from Iran and Syria along with substantial non-state support and has been designated a Foreign Terrorist Organization (FTO), a Specially Designated Terrorist (SDT), and a Specially Designated Global Terrorist (SDGT) by the U.S. government.[1]

On May 4, 2011, in Cairo, Egypt, Mahmoud Abbas and Hamas political bureau chief Khaled Meshaal signed a Fatah-Hamas PA power-sharing agreement brokered by Egypt intended to bridge the Palestinian geographical and factional divide and to clear the way for PA presidential and parliamentary elections in a year's time. This could also present a unified Palestinian stance in international negotiations and fora and may have a significant impact on Israeli-Palestinian relations. Analysts are vigorously debating both what the Fatah-Hamas deal signifies about each party's motivations and leverage over the other, as well as what it signifies about greater regional implications given the ongoing political change and unrest around Israel, the West Bank, and Gaza—particularly in Egypt and Syria.

Reports indicate that Fatah and Hamas have agreed to allow a "technocratic" PA government— presumably run by ministers without formal party affiliations—until such time as elections can be held. The factions have also agreed to form a Higher Security Committee under Abbas's leadership, but almost no actual details about how West Bank and Gaza security forces might coordinate have been publicly communicated.

Whether the possible benefits to Palestinians of fully implementing a power-sharing deal can persuade Fatah and Hamas to overcome their deep differences and distrust of one another, along with their reluctance to risk their respective power bases and claims to legitimacy, is unclear, as is whether any such deal might meet the conditions of the United States and other members of the international Quartet (European Union, United Nations, Russia) regarding international dealings with and aid to a Palestinian entity that includes Hamas in some manner.[2] Decisions by international donors, including resource-rich Gulf Arab states, could influence Israel's willingness to continue transferring tax and customs revenues it collects on behalf of the PA, as well as how the PA chooses to configure its governing, security, and electoral arrangements. For information on legal conditions on U.S. aid to a PA power-sharing government, see "Major Conditions, Limitations, and Restrictions on Aid," below.

From FY2008 to the present, annual U.S. bilateral assistance to the West Bank and Gaza Strip has averaged over $600 million, including annual averages of over $200 million in direct budgetary assistance and over $100 million in non-lethal security assistance for the PA in the West Bank. The remainder—approximately $300 million on average per year—is dedicated to project assistance for the West Bank and Gaza through U.S. government grants to non-governmental organizations (NGOs). Much of this assistance is in direct support of PA Prime Minister Salam Fayyad's security, governance, development, and reform programs aimed at building Palestinian institutions in advance of statehood. The post-2007 annual average of U.S. bilateral assistance is substantially greater than the approximate annual average of $170 million from 2000-2007 and $70 million from 1994-1999. Despite more robust levels of assistance, the absence of Israeli-Palestinian peace and Hamas's heightened role in Palestinian politics could make effective implementation of lasting aid projects difficult.

Because of congressional concerns that, among other things, U.S. funds might be diverted to Palestinian terrorist groups, this aid is subject to a host of vetting and oversight requirements and legislative restrictions (see "Major Conditions, Limitations, and Restrictions on Aid" below). U.S. assistance to the Palestinians is given alongside assistance from other international donors, and U.S. policymakers routinely call for greater or more timely assistance from Arab governments in line with their pledges.

Additional U.S. humanitarian assistance for Palestinian refugees in Gaza and elsewhere continues through contributions to the U.N. Relief and Works Agency for Palestine Refugees in the Near East (UNRWA). U.S. contributions to UNRWA, which have totaled approximately $4 billion since UNRWA's inception in 1950, have averaged over $200 million annually since 2007.

HISTORICAL BACKGROUND AND RECENT DEVELOPMENTS

Since the establishment of limited Palestinian self-rule in the West Bank and Gaza Strip in the mid-1990s, the U.S. government has committed more than $4 billion in bilateral assistance to the Palestinians in the West Bank and Gaza,[3] who are among the largest per capita recipients of foreign aid worldwide.[4] This assistance has focused on the further development of the Palestinian economic, social services, and civil society sectors; and on strengthening the processes, governance, and security-providing capacities of Palestinian Authority (PA) institutions, through partnerships with U.S. and Palestinian organizations.

Following the death of Yasser Arafat in 2004 and his succession by Mahmoud Abbas as PA President in 2005, Congress and the Bush Administration increased U.S. assistance to the Palestinians. However, when the 2006 Hamas victory in Palestinian Legislative Council elections reversed the renewed sense of U.S. optimism in elected Palestinian leadership, U.S. assistance was restructured and reduced. The United States halted direct foreign aid to the PA but continued providing humanitarian and project assistance to the Palestinian people through international and non-governmental organizations (NGOs). The ban on direct assistance continued during the brief tenure of a Hamas-led power-sharing government (February to June 2007). During that time, the United States and the other members of the international Quartet (the United Nations, the European Union, and Russia) unsuccessfully demanded that Hamas accept the Quartet principles—recognition of Israel's right to exist, renunciation of violence, and acceptance of previous Israeli-Palestinian agreements.

Subsequent events altered the situation dramatically. In June 2007, Hamas forcibly took control of the Gaza Strip.[5] PA President and Fatah head Mahmoud Abbas, calling the move a "coup," dissolved the power-sharing government and tasked the politically independent technocrat Salam Fayyad to serve as prime minister and organize a new PA "caretaker" government in the West Bank. Within days, the United States lifted its economic and political embargo on the PA.

The Bush Administration and Congress then boosted U.S. aid levels in hopes of fostering an economic and security climate conducive to peaceful coexistence between Israel and a future Palestinian state. The revival of Israeli-Palestinian negotiations for a final-status agreement in conjunction with the Annapolis Conference of November 2007 provided further impetus for U.S. economic support of the institutional and societal building blocks deemed crucial for Palestinian self-governance. The Obama Administration has advocated a similar approach. Attempts by both Administrations to broker an Israeli-Palestinian negotiating process that yields a substantive and lasting resolution of core issues in dispute by the parties (borders, security, refugees, the status of Jerusalem, settlements, and water rights) have thus far proven unsuccessful.

Following the Fatah-Hamas power-sharing agreement, prospects for negotiations may be even dimmer for the near term given heightened Israeli security concerns in the context of region-wide political uncertainty and plans by the PA and Palestine Liberation Organization (PLO) to pursue widespread international recognition of Palestinian statehood, including possibly through a resolution at the United Nations General Assembly in September 2011.

Major Conditions, Limitations, and Restrictions on Aid

Annual appropriations legislation routinely contains the following conditions, limitations, and restrictions on U.S. aid to Palestinians:[6]

- *Hamas*: No aid is permitted for Hamas or Hamas-controlled entities.
- *Power-Sharing PA Government*: No aid is permitted for a power-sharing PA government that includes Hamas as a member unless the President certifies that the PA government, including all ministers, has accepted the following two principles embodied in Section 620K of the Palestinian Anti-Terrorism Act of 2006 (PATA), P.L. 109-446: (1) recognition of "the Jewish state of Israel's right to exist" and (2) acceptance of previous Israeli-Palestinian agreements (the "Section

620K principles"). If the PA government is "Hamas-controlled," PATA applies additional conditions, limitations, and restrictions on aid. Under PATA, in the event Hamas participation in a PA government precludes ministries from receiving aid, the PA President and judiciary (if not Hamas-controlled) may under certain conditions receive aid pursuant to a presidential waiver for national security purposes.

It is unclear whether a "technocratic" government of the type anticipated under the May 2011 Fatah-Hamas power-sharing arrangement—whose ministers are not formally aligned with Hamas—would come under the legal definition of a "power-sharing PA government that includes Hamas as a member" or a "Hamas-controlled" PA government and thus trigger these additional conditions on U.S. aid. Under PATA, the Palestinian Legislative Council (PLC) is considered to be part of the PA, but the legal consequences if the PLC were to reconvene with the majority Hamas won in 2006 are still unclear.[7]

- *PLO and Palestinian Broadcasting Corporation (PBC)*: No aid is permitted for the PLO or for the PBC.
- *Palestinian State*: No aid is permitted for a future Palestinian state unless the Secretary of State certifies that the governing entity of the state

1) has demonstrated a firm commitment to peaceful coexistence with the State of Israel;
2) is taking appropriate measures to counter terrorism and terrorist financing in the West Bank and Gaza in cooperation with Israel and others; and
3) is working with other countries in the region to vigorously pursue efforts to establish a just, lasting, and comprehensive peace in the Middle East that will enable Israel and an independent Palestinian state to exist within the context of full and normal relationships.

This restriction does not apply to aid meant to reform the Palestinian governing entity so that it might meet the three conditions outlined above. Additionally, the President is permitted to waive this restriction for national security purposes.

- *PA Personnel in Gaza*: No aid is permitted for PA personnel located in Gaza. Although the PA does pay salaries to individuals located in

Gaza, USAID says that U.S. direct budgetary assistance to the PA goes toward paying off the PA's commercial debts (see "Direct Assistance to the Palestinian Authority" below).

- *Vetting, Monitoring, and Evaluation*: As discussed throughout this report, for U.S. aid programs for the Palestinians, annual appropriations legislation routinely requires executive branch reports and certifications, as well as internal and Government Accountability Office (GAO) audits. These requirements are aimed at preventing U.S. aid from benefitting Palestinian terrorists or abetting corruption, ensuring the amenability of Palestinian society and institutions to aid programs, assessing the programs' effectiveness, and monitoring intervening variables (such as aid from international actors).[8]

TYPES OF U.S. BILATERAL AID TO THE PALESTINIANS

Table 1. U.S. Bilateral Assistance to the Palestinians, FY2005-FY2012 (regular and supplemental appropriations; current year $ in millions)

Account	FY2005	FY2006	FY2007	FY2008	FY2009	FY2010	FY2011	FY2012[a]
ESF	224.4	148.5	50.0	389.5	776.0	400.4	400.4	400.4
P.L. 480	6.0	4.4	19.488	-	20.715	-	-	-
Title II								
(Food Aid)								
INCLE[b]	-	-	-	25.0	184.0	100.0	150.0	113.0
Total	230.4	153.243	69.488	414.5	980.715	502.9	550.4	513.4

Sources: U.S. State Department, USAID.

Notes: All amounts are approximate; for purposes of this table and this report, "bilateral assistance" does not include U.S. contributions to UNRWA or other international organizations from the Migration and Refugee Assistance (MRA) or Emergency Refugee and Migration Assistance (ERMA) accounts, regardless of how the term is defined in legislation.

[a] Amounts stated for FY2012 have been requested but not yet appropriated.

[b]. INCLE stands for International Narcotics Control and Law Enforcement. INCLE figures do not include $86.362 million of FY2006 ESF funds reprogrammed into the INCLE account by President Bush in January 2007 (see "Direct Assistance to the Palestinian Authority" below).

Table 2. Proposed Spending Plan for FY2012 Bilateral Assistance

Amount	Purpose
Economic Support Fund ($400.4 million total)	
$200 million	Direct budgetary assistance to Palestinian Authority (PA) in West Bank
$200.4 million	Assistance for the West Bank and Gaza (through USAID)[a]
	• $20 million – governance, rule of law, civil society
	• $79.7 million – health, education, social services
	• $53.2 million – economic development
	• $47.5 million – humanitarian assistance
International Narcotics Control and Law Enforcement ($113 million total)	
$77 million	Training, non-lethal equipment, and garrisoning assistance to PA security forces in the West Bank, supporting efforts by the U.S. Security Coordinator
$36 million	Assistance for PA Ministry of Interior and for the justice sector (prosecutors and criminal investigators) to improve performance, efficiency, and interinstitutional cooperation
	Rule-of-law infrastructure, including courthouses, police stations, and prisons

Source: U.S. State Department, FY2012 Congressional Budget Justification for Foreign Operations (Annex: Regional Perspectives), available at http://www.state

Notes: All amounts are approximate. a. See footnote 10.

Economic Support Fund Project Assistance

Types of Funding Programs

Most aid to the Palestinians is appropriated through the Economic Support Fund (ESF) account and provided by USAID (and, to a far lesser degree, the State Department[9]) to U.S. nongovernmental organizations (NGOs) operating in the West Bank and the Gaza Strip.[10] Funds are allocated in this program for projects in sectors such as humanitarian assistance, economic development, democratic reform, improving water access and other infrastructure, health care, education, and vocational training (currently most, if not all, funds for the Gaza Strip are dedicated to humanitarian assistance and economic recovery needs).[11] See Table 2 above for the Obama Administration's proposed spending plan for FY2012 ESF West Bank/Gaza assistance.

Vetting Requirements and Procedures

USAID subjects its programs worldwide to vetting requirements to ensure the proper use of funds appropriated through its accounts. USAID's West Bank and Gaza program is subject to a specialized vetting process (for non-U.S. organizations) and to yearly audits intended to ensure that funds are not diverted to Hamas or other organizations classified as terrorist groups by the U.S. government.[12] This vetting process has become more rigorous in recent years in response to allegations that U.S. economic assistance was indirectly supporting Palestinian terrorist groups, and following an internal audit in which USAID concluded it could not "reasonably ensure" that its money would not wind up in terrorist hands.[13]

A February 2009 statement from USAID described its revamped vetting procedures as follows:

> All NGOs applying for grants from USAID are required to certify, before award of the grant will be made, that they do not provide material support to terrorists.... Before making an award of either a contract or a grant to a local NGO, the USAID West Bank/Gaza Mission checks the organization and its principal officers, directors and other key personnel against lists maintained by the Office of Foreign Assets Control (OFAC) within the U.S. Department of Treasury. The Mission also checks these organizations and individuals through law enforcement and intelligence community systems accessed by USAID's Office of Security. At present, the Mission collects additional information up front in addition to the individual's full [four-part] name, such as a government issued photo-ID number and the individual's date and place of birth.... [USAID's] West Bank/Gaza program possess[es] the most comprehensive partner vetting system for foreign assistance throughout the U.S. Government.[14]

A May 2009 Government Accountability Office (GAO) report found that USAID had strengthened its antiterrorism policies and procedures in response to recommendations GAO had made in a 2006 report.[15]

Direct Assistance to the Palestinian Authority

Budgetary assistance is a major part of the U.S. strategy to support the PA in the West Bank, although some Members of Congress expect better governance and more vigilant action from the PA towards peace with Israel in return.[16] According to annual foreign operations appropriations laws, congressionally approved funds for the West Bank and Gaza Strip cannot be given directly to the PA unless the President submits a waiver to Congress stating that doing so is in the interest of national security, and the Secretary of State certifies that there is a single PA treasury account, civil service roster, and payroll.[17] Annual appropriations legislation also routinely caps direct U.S. budgetary assistance to the PA (the cap for FY2011 is $200 million under P.L. 112-10, the Department of Defense and Continuing Appropriations Act, 2011) and places conditions on aid to any power-sharing PA government "of which Hamas is a member" (for further discussion, see "Hamas and a "Unity Government"?" below). Even after money is transferred to the PA's treasury account, the United States retains prior approval of any transactions from that account, along with a three-year power of audit over those funds.[18]

During the final year of President George W. Bush's Administration, President Bush issued waivers providing $300 million in direct budgetary assistance to the PA. President Barack Obama has followed the precedent Bush established by authorizing a total of $500 million in direct budgetary assistance during his first two years in office, as follows:

- In July 2009, $200 million in ESF money were transferred to the PA in the wake of a presidential waiver issued by President Obama.[19]
- In November 2009, $75 million in budgetary assistance were provided to the PA under the July presidential waiver as an advance on FY2010 ESF funds, pursuant to a continuing resolution (later appropriated pursuant to P.L. 111-117).
- In April 2010, another $75 million in budgetary assistance from the ESF account were provided to the PA via presidential waiver.[20]
- In November 2010, $150 million in budgetary assistance were provided to the PA via presidential waiver as an advance on FY2011 ESF funds, pursuant to the Continuing Appropriations Act, 2011 (P.L. 111-242).[21]

Direct U.S. budgetary assistance to the PA goes toward paying off its commercial debt, as the following USAID congressional notification language says:

> Cash transfer funds will be used in the same manner as previous transfers - to service debt to commercial suppliers and commercial banks. Debt to commercial banks will be debt originally incurred for purchases from commercial suppliers. Each of the payees will be vetted in accordance with USAID West Bank and Gaza existing procedures, as applicable, as a precondition to the transfer of funds by the PA for such payments. Funds may also be used to pay for upcoming purchases from commercial suppliers or reimbursements of recent purchases from the same.[22]

U.S. Security Assistance to the Palestinian Authority[23]

As mentioned above, aid has been given to train, reform, advise, house, and provide non-lethal equipment for PA civil security forces in the West Bank loyal to President Abbas in an effort both to counter militants from organizations such as Hamas and Palestinian Islamic Jihad, and to establish the rule of law for an expected Palestinian state. A small amount of training assistance also has been provided to strengthen and reform the PA criminal justice sector. This assistance has come from the International Narcotics Control and Law Enforcement (INCLE) account—to which a total of $545.4 million has been appropriated or reprogrammed for use in the West Bank since 2007. The Obama Administration has requested an additional $113 million in FY2012 INCLE funding (see *Table 2* above).

Since Hamas gained control of the Gaza Strip, the U.S. Security Coordinator (USSC) for Israel and the Palestinian Authority (a three-star U.S. general, supported by U.S. and allied staff and military officers from the United Kingdom, Canada, and Turkey) has worked in coordination with the State Department's Bureau of International Narcotics and Law Enforcement Affairs (INL) to help train roughly 1,000 PA Presidential Guard and 3,700 PA National Security Forces (NSF) troops at the International Police Training Center near Amman, Jordan. The USSC and INL reportedly plan to help organize and train a total of approximately 6,000 troops, including 10 500-man NSF battalions (approximately 7 of which have already been trained or begun training).

This U.S. assistance program exists alongside other assistance and training programs reportedly provided to Palestinian security forces and intelligence organizations by the European Union and various countries, including probable covert U.S. assistance programs.[24] By most accounts, the PA forces receiving training have shown increased professionalism and have helped substantially improve law and order and lower the profile of terrorist organizations in West Bank cities.

However, the aspiration to coordinate international security assistance efforts and to consolidate the various PA security forces under unified civilian control that is accountable to rule of law and to human rights norms remains largely unfulfilled. PA forces have come under criticism for the political targeting of Hamas—in collaboration with Israel and the United States—through massive shutdowns and forced leadership changes to West Bank charities with alleged ties to Hamas members and through reportedly arbitrary detentions of Hamas members and supporters.[25] Some Palestinians and outside observers also assert that the effectiveness and credibility of PA operations are undermined by Israeli restrictions—including curfews, checkpoints, no-go zones, and limitations on international arms and equipment transfers—as well as by Israel's own security operations in the West Bank[26] and the blockade and closure of crossings around Gaza. Israel claims that its continuing operations in the West Bank are necessary in order to reduce the threat of terrorism. It is unclear how concerns about the effectiveness of the PA security might evolve if anti-Israel protests in the West Bank increase in frequency and intensity amid the region-wide political unrest and heightened Israeli-Palestinian tension.

How the May 2011 Fatah-Hamas power-sharing agreement may affect the activities of PA security forces in the West Bank is unclear, although it is possible that these activities will remain largely unchanged until either PA presidential and legislative elections can be held or Fatah and Hamas can agree on security coordination for both the West Bank and Gaza. The likelihood of either contingency occurring is seriously questioned by many observers.

U.S. Contributions to UNRWA

Overview

The United States is the largest single-state donor to UNRWA, which provides food, shelter, medical care, and education for many of the original refugees from the 1948 Arab-Israeli war and their descendants—now comprising approximately 4.8 million Palestinians in Jordan, Syria, Lebanon, the West Bank, and Gaza. U.S. contributions to UNRWA—separate from U.S. bilateral aid to the West Bank and Gaza—come from the Migration and Refugee Assistance (MRA) account and the Emergency Refugee and Migration Assistance (ERMA) account. Since UNRWA's inception in 1950, the United States has provided the agency with approximately $4 billion in contributions (see Table 3 below). Other refugees worldwide fall under the mandate of the U.N. High Commissioner for Refugees (UNHCR).

The budget for UNRWA's core activities (general fund) in 2009 was $545.6 million, funded mainly by Western governments, international organizations, and private donors.[27] UNRWA also creates special emergency funds for pressing humanitarian needs, such as in the wake of the 2008-2009 Gaza conflict. U.S. contributions (which are made from the Migration and Refugee Assistance (MRA) and Emergency Refugee and Migration Assistance (ERMA) accounts managed by the State Department's Bureau of Population, Refugees, and Migration (PRM)) totaled $238 million for FY2010 ($125 million for the general fund, $113 for emergency funds and special projects), and totaled $268 million for FY2009 ($116 and $152 million, respectively) and $185 million for FY2008 ($100 and $85 million, respectively).

Until the 1990s, Arab governments refrained from contributing to UNRWA's budget in an effort to keep the Palestinian refugee issue on the international agenda and to press Israel to accept responsibility for their plight. Since then, most Arab states have made relatively small annual contributions.

In Gaza, most observers acknowledge that the role of UNRWA in providing basic services (i.e., food, health care, education) takes much of the governing burden off Hamas. As a result, some complain that this amounts to UNRWA's enabling of Hamas and argue that its activities should be discontinued or scaled back. This is in addition to critics who question UNRWA's existence because they believe it perpetuates Palestinian dependency and resentment against Israel.[28] However, many others, U.S. and Israeli officials included, believe that UNRWA plays a valuable role by providing stability and serving as the eyes and ears of the international community in Gaza. They generally prefer UNRWA to the uncertain alternative that might emerge if UNRWA were removed from the picture.[29]

Table 3. Historical U.S. Government Contributions to UNRWA (in $ millions)

Fiscal Year(s)	Amount	Fiscal Year(s)	Amount
1950-1989	1,473.3	2000	89.0
1990	57.0	2001	123.0
1991	75.6	2002	119.3
1992	69.0	2003	134.0
1993	73.8	2004	127.4
1994	78.2	2005	108.0
1995	74.8	2006	137.0
1996	77.0	2007	154.2
1997	79.2	2008	184.7
1998	78.3	2009	268.0
1999	80.5	2010	237.8
		TOTAL	**3,899.1**

Source: U.S. State Department Notes: All amounts are approximate.

Issues for Congress

Some observers, including a former general counsel for UNRWA, have criticized UNRWA for, among other things, insufficient or flawed vetting procedures and engaging in political advocacy.[30] UNRWA and its supporters, however, maintain that UNRWA officials are fulfilling their mandated roles as well as can be expected under challenging circumstances (i.e., UNRWA's lack of a robust policing capability and other operational limitations, political pressures, security concerns).[31]

In testimony before the House Appropriations Subcommittee on State, Foreign Operations and Related Programs on April 23, 2009, Secretary of State Hillary Rodham Clinton spoke for the Obama Administration regarding U.S. oversight of contributions to UNRWA:

> We have made it clear to UNRWA, the United Nations Relief And Works Agency, that we intend to carefully track any aid that they receive.

> They have taken additional steps, partly at our urging, to make their process more transparent, consistent with both United Nations commitments and U.S. legislation. They conduct background checks on employees. They share staff lists with us and with Israel. They prohibit staff participation in political activities. They launch investigations upon receiving information from Israel, us, or anyone else about any staff member engaging in inappropriate or illicit activities. They are actually investigating staff members right now who were elected in internal elections within Gaza. And we have pressed them very hard because they have to earn our confidence in this.[32]

Vetting of UNRWA Contributions

The primary concern raised by some Members of Congress is that U.S. contributions to UNRWA might be used to support terrorists. Section 301(c) of the 1961 Foreign Assistance Act (P.L. 87- 195), as amended, says that "No contributions by the United States shall be made to [UNRWA] except on the condition that [UNRWA] take[s] all possible measures to assure that no part of the United States contribution shall be used to furnish assistance to any refugee who is receiving military training as a member of the so-called Palestine Liberation Army or any other guerrilla type organization or who has engaged in any act of terrorism."

A May 2009 GAO report said that, since a previous GAO report in 2003, UNRWA and the State Department had strengthened their policies and procedures to conform with Section 301(c) legal requirements, but that "weaknesses remain."[33] Neither report found UNRWA to be in noncompliance with Section 301(c), and to date, no arm of the U.S. government has made such a finding. The following are some points from the 2009 report and subsequent developments related to it:

- In the 2009 GAO report, State officials said compliance is evaluated based on State's "internal level of confidence that UNRWA has taken all possible measures to ensure that terrorists are not receiving assistance, such as having procedures in place and taking measures to respond to issues that arise."[34] State has not defined the term "all possible measures," nor has it defined what would constitute noncompliance with Section 301(c).
- The report said that State had not established written criteria to use in evaluating UNRWA's compliance with Section 301(c), and recommended that State consider doing so.[35] In November 2009, State and UNRWA signed a non-binding "Framework for Cooperation" for

2010. The document agreed that, along with the compliance reports UNRWA submits to State biannually, State would use 15 enumerated criteria "as a way to evaluate" UNRWA's compliance with Section 301(c). State signed a similar document with UNRWA for 2011.[36]

- UNRWA said that it screens its staff and contractors every six months and that it screened all 4.6 million Palestinian refugees and microfinance clients in December 2008 (and intends to make this a routine procedure) for terrorist ties to Al Qaeda and the Taliban, pursuant to a list established pursuant to U.N. Security Council Resolution 1267. UNRWA said that it is unable to screen those of its beneficiaries who are displaced persons from the 1967 war because it does not collect information on those persons.[37]
- UNRWA's UN 1267 terrorist screening list does not include Hamas, Hezbollah, or most other militant groups that operate in UNRWA's surroundings. UNRWA is unwilling to screen its contractors and funding recipients against a list supplied by only one U.N. member state. Nevertheless, UNRWA officials did say that if notified by U.S. officials of potential matches, they would "use the information as a trigger to conduct their own investigation," which led to the report's recommendation that the State Department consider screening UNRWA contractors.[38] In response, State says that it now screens quarterly, against the Excluded Parties Lists System (EPLS, which is a list of parties excluded throughout the U.S. government from receiving federal contracts[39]),

the names of vendors of contracts equal to or exceeding $100,000, as provided by UNRWA. Each of UNRWA's 83 contract awardees of over $100,000 for the 2nd Quarter (April-June 2010) was screened twice by separate PRM staff. The analysis resulted in no matches against the EPLS.[40]

- UNRWA has established procedures to investigate inappropriate staff behavior. UNRWA [said] that it seeks information from authorities whenever staff are detained, convicted, or refused a permit or targeted by Israeli military forces. UNRWA officials said they share the names of all UNRWA staff annually with the governments of Egypt, Israel, Jordan, Lebanon, Syria, and the Palestinian Authority but have received no information on staff members from these governments.[41]
- UNRWA officials said that UNRWA provides assistance "in the context of its humanitarian mandate, meaning that agency policy is

> generally not to deny education or primary healthcare benefits." The officials said that if a refugee was denied benefits because of suspected militant or terrorist activities or ties, his or her child "would not be disqualified from attending an UNRWA school."[42]

Resettlement of Palestinian Refugees from Iraq

According to the State Department as of August 2010, the only Palestinian refugees being resettled in the United States were from Iraq:

> Since 2008, 679 Palestinians from Iraq have arrived for resettlement in nearly all 50 states across the U.S. through the U.S. Refugee Admissions Program (USRAP). PRM expects additional arrivals over the next two months, thus this number will increase by the end of this fiscal year. [The United Nations High Commissioner for Refugees (UNHCR)] referred 1,350 Palestinians to the USRAP for resettlement in [the United States] since FY2008. Processing of this group has taken place in two locations: at the Al Waleed camp located on the Iraqi-Syrian border and in the International Zone in Baghdad. The USRAP will process more Palestinians for resettlement if they are referred by UNHCR.[43]

The State Department says that it has not contributed to the resettlement costs of Palestinian refugees from Iraq.[44] According to the website of the U.S. Citizenship and Immigration Services bureau of the Department of Homeland Security, refugees relocating to the United States generally receive loans from the International Organization for Migration for their transportation expenses. They are "expected to repay the cost of their transportation once they are established in the United States."[45]

The State Department has said that Palestinian refugees from Iraq who are potentially relocating to the United States are screened for potential security risks.

> Palestinians from Iraq undergo screening as if they were Iraqi citizens, including the enhanced security checks undergone by all Iraqi refugee applicants. These procedures consist of name and biometric checks against various additional U.S. Government databases to ensure that the applicants pose no known security risks.[46]

The State Department made $4.7 million in FY2009 and FY2010 "special project" contributions (from the MRA account) to UNRWA specifically dedicated to assisting Palestinian refugees from Iraq who have relocated to Syria. According to State, "While Palestinians from Iraq fall under UNHCR's mandate, UNHCR and UNRWA closely coordinate assistance to this population to allow Palestinians from Iraq to access services from either agency as many families live on the outskirts of Palestinian refugee camps and do not feel safe traveling to UNHCR's office. In 2009 UNHCR and UNRWA established a joint registration process for Palestinians from Iraq in order to ensure that families are not receiving the same assistance from both agencies."[47] The special project contributions provide the refugees with basic services such as food, education, and emergency shelter.[48]

Legislation

Critiques of UNRWA's operations are routinely raised, and some Members of Congress have supported legislation or resolutions aimed at increasing oversight of the agency, strengthening its vetting procedures, and/or capping U.S. contributions. H.Rept. 111-151 contained a provision from the joint explanatory statement capping contributions to UNRWA at $119 million for its operations in the West Bank and Gaza from FY2009 funds appropriated pursuant to P.L. 111-32. This provision also required a report from the Secretary of State to the Committees on Appropriations no later than 45 days following the enactment of P.L. 111-32 on various UNRWA self-policing and transparency-promoting activities, including measures UNRWA takes to comply with Section 301(c) of the 1961 Foreign Assistance Act relating to preventing assistance to terrorists.[49] P.L. 111-117 (incorporated by reference in the relevant particulars for FY2011 by P.L. 112-10) contains the same reporting requirement, without an accompanying cap on contributions.

ISSUES FOR CONGRESS IN DETERMINING FUTURE AID

Hamas and a "Unity Government"?

Although Fatah and Hamas reached an Egyptian-facilitated power-sharing agreement in May 2011, questions over how the agreement might actually be implemented persist. These questions include how PA and Hamas security operations might be integrated, when and how Palestinian presidential and legislative elections might be conducted, and who might occupy PA government positions. Proposed resolutions were introduced in May 2011 in both the House (H.Res. 268) and Senate (S.Res. 185) questioning the continuation of U.S. aid to a PA government that includes Hamas, although the resolutions do not expressly address whether they contemplate that

Hamas's underlying approval of a PA government that includes formally non-aligned "technocrats" instead of Hamas members would be sufficient to connote its involvement in the government.[50]

As mentioned above (see "Major Conditions, Limitations, and Restrictions on Aid"), current appropriations legislation prohibits the United States from providing financial assistance to Hamas under any conditions. This law also prohibits U.S. assistance to a PA government with Hamas ministers (subject to possible exceptions for a non-Hamas PA president and judiciary) unless all the government's ministers accept the "Section 620K principles": (1) recognition of "the Jewish state of Israel's right to exist" and (2) acceptance of previous Israeli-Palestinian agreements—named after the section in PATA (P.L. 109-446) that sets them forth. These principles have some similarity to the principles the so-called international Quartet (United States, European Union, United Nations, and Russia) has required Hamas to meet before accepting dealings with it: (1) recognizing Israel's right to exist, (2) renouncing violence, and (3) accepting previous Israeli-Palestinian agreements.

Future debates might focus on the following issues:

- Whether to relax or tighten U.S. restrictions on which Palestinian party/ies should be answerable for accepting and complying with the Section 620K principles.
- Whether to grant the U.S. President discretion—under certain conditions and/or for specific purposes—to waive aid restrictions relating to a power-sharing government that includes Hamas and does not meet the Section 620K principles.

Secretary of State Hillary Rodham Clinton gave testimony at an April 2009 congressional hearing regarding the possibility of Hamas members serving in a PA government that would accept the Quartet principles and/or the Section 620K principles. At the time, she stated that "we are currently funding the Lebanese government, which has Hezbollah in it" because of a U.S. interest in supporting a government working to prevent the "further incursion of extremism."[51]

Assuming that the United States chooses not to engage with and/or contribute to a PA government that includes Hamas, future debates might take place over the degree to which the United States should actively dissuade others in the international community—particularly European and Arab actors—from engagement and contributions.[52]

Questions Regarding a Two-State Solution

Even assuming that the immediate objectives of U.S. assistance to the Palestinians—relieving humanitarian needs in Gaza and improving security and facilitating development in the West Bank—are met, a failure to achieve progress towards a politically legitimate and peaceful two-state solution could undermine the utility of U.S. aid in helping the Palestinians become more cohesive, stable, and self-reliant over the long term.

Many factors may complicate prospects for a negotiated two-state solution:

- Discord within and among Palestinian factions—reflected geographically by (unless and until the May 2011 power-sharing agreement is implemented) divided rule in the West Bank and Gaza and ideologically by Hamas's refusal to join the PLO in forswearing violent resistance against Israel.
- Conditions that the Israeli government in power since April 2009 under Prime Minister Binyamin Netanyahu has attached to any consideration on its part of the concept of an independent Palestinian state, such as demilitarization and recognition of Israel as the "nation state of the Jewish people."[53]
- Physical entrenchment of Israeli settlers in the West Bank and of obstacles to Palestinian movement within the West Bank and in and out of both the West Bank and Gaza, together with its political and socioeconomic consequences.
- Possibility of course-changing events—such as a major terrorist attack, a surprise election outcome, an outbreak of war, or pursuit by Palestinians of a political pathway to statehood as an alternative to negotiations with Israel.[54] This possibility could be exacerbated by the region-wide unrest and political change that has been ongoing since early 2011.

The proposed resolutions discussed above (with regard to a possible power-sharing PA government) that were introduced in May 2011 in both the House (H.Res. 268) and Senate (S.Res. 185) indicate that some Members of Congress might consider curtailing aid to the Palestinian Authority and possibly other aid to the Palestinians in the event the PLO/PA seeks to circumvent negotiations with Israel through appeals to the United Nations, other international bodies or fora, and/or foreign governments for recognition of statehood or similar diplomatic support.[55]

The Gaza Situation

Hamas's control of Gaza presents a conundrum for many. Most parties, including Israel and the PA, are concerned that assisting Gaza's population and rebuilding infrastructure damaged during Operation Cast Lead (the 2008-2009 Israel-Hamas conflict) could bolster Hamas. Thus, while controlled levels of humanitarian assistance have been permitted to enter Gaza, reconstruction projects have been very limited.[56] In June and December 2010, Israel announced plans to ease the closure regime it has enforced at its crossings with Gaza. More goods have come into Gaza as a result, but it is not clear if, when, and under what conditions a full resumption of agricultural and industrial trade and movement of persons between Gaza and the outside world might be expected. In late May 2011, Egypt permanently opened its crossing with Gaza at Rafah to passenger traffic, but because this will not extend to the passage of goods, it might not have a material effect on trade and smuggling patterns. Many observers believe that either Hamas's positions on the Quartet principles or its control over Gaza would have to change before substantial U.S. funds might be used in the reconstruction of buildings and infrastructure in Gaza, with the exception of U.N. facilities and other special cases such as international schools.[57] In the meantime, occasional skirmishes between Palestinian militants (including Hamas) and Israel along Gaza's borders and continuing low-level rocket and mortar fire from Gaza at targets in Israel could spiral into renewed conflict.

Members of Congress are routinely wary that bilateral assistance for Gaza or contributions to UNRWA could be misused and diverted to benefit Hamas or other terrorist groups. Yet, some Members of Congress advocate expanding the level and type of humanitarian and development assistance to Gaza—often at the same time they advocate easing, ending, or even challenging the Israeli-Egyptian closure regime—because Gazans are seen as needing more support to improve their economic, physical, and psychological situations. In January 2010, 54 Representatives from the 111th Congress signed a letter to President Obama that requested a substantive lifting of the closure regime.[58]

Strengthening the PA in the West Bank

Instability in the West Bank and the Gaza Strip is, paradoxically, both a major reason for the increases in U.S. assistance over the past three years and a factor that could lead some to oppose maintaining or boosting current aid levels. After Hamas's takeover of the Gaza Strip and dismissal from the PA in June 2007, the United States made assisting the PA with economic development and civil security—aimed at bolstering the standing of President Abbas and the Fayyad government—a higher priority. Yet, if the PA in Ramallah proves unable, at a minimum, to achieve and maintain popular legitimacy and competent control in the West Bank, U.S. reluctance to provide resources and training might increase, given concerns that aid could be used against Israel or Palestinian civilians, either by falling into the hands of Hamas or otherwise. Some observers argue that U.S. assistance does not enhance the legitimacy of Abbas and the PA, but rather detracts from it by leading some Palestinians to conclude that the PA is too beholden to the United States.[59] Others have warned that U.S. dependence on individual leaders such as Abbas and Fayyad works against long-term stability by undermining mechanisms of democratic governance and enabling growing authoritarianism.[60] The May 2011 Fatah-Hamas power-sharing agreement might also raise concerns that PA leaders may be insufficiently strong or motivated to prevent Hamas from gaining greater influence in the West Bank.

Economic Development and International Donor Assistance

The appointment in June 2007 of Salam Fayyad, a former World Bank and International Monetary Fund official, as PA prime minister raised hopes for Palestinian reform and economic growth that have been realized in part. Fayyad has produced reform proposals aimed at establishing a "de facto Palestinian state"[61] that have helped garner major international donor assistance pledges and promises of investment. International pledges of support, however, have routinely proven insufficient to cover the PA's budgetary expenses, occasionally requiring efforts by Fayyad to obtain last-minute assistance and/or private financing. The success of Fayyad's reform plans appears to hinge on the following factors:

- Keeping the public sector solvent enough to sustain long-term private sector development;

- Getting Israeli restrictions loosened or lifted on the movement of goods and people both within and out of the West Bank and Gaza[62] and on Palestinian development projects in so-called "Area C";[63] and
- Overall political progress to overcome Palestinian factional /geographical division and towards Palestinian statehood.[64]

Several high-profile projects—housing developments, industrial parks, superstores, entertainment complexes—have been completed or are in various stages of proposal or construction in and around Ramallah, Bethlehem, Jericho, and the northern West Bank in an effort to jumpstart private sector development.[65] The World Bank reported real GDP growth of 9.3% for the West Bank and Gaza in 2010.[66] Yet, most analysts assert that actual and prospective economic development should not be overstated because the West Bank economy continues to be propped up by external aid and continues to recover from historic economic lows precipitated by the conflicts of the past decade (see Figure 1 below). Furthermore, uncertainty remains regarding movement and access and regarding progress in negotiations with Israel.[67]

Fayyad's future status within the PA government, and possibly the continuing prospects of Western support for the reform and economic development programs described above, have been thrown into limbo pending formation of the new government under the May 2011 Fatah-Hamas power-sharing agreement.

Congress has indicated its interest in staying abreast of the economic assistance Arab states provide to the West Bank and the PA, sometimes requiring reports from the Administration on the subject.[68] Arab states (especially Gulf states) provided large amounts of aid to the Hamas-led PA government in 2006-2007 after the United States and European Union withdrew their aid, but following the reinstitution of U.S. and EU aid in mid-2007, most of them reduced contributions.[69] Routinely, they make generous pledges (including over $1.8 billion dollars in the wake of the 2008-2009 Gaza conflict) of aid to the Palestinians, but at times fulfill them only in part and after significant delay. Their reluctance to fulfill pledges may stem from misgivings over "picking sides" in Palestinian factional disputes and from concerns that without imminent prospects either for domestic political unity or for progress on the peace process, any money contributed could be a waste. On the part of the Gulf states in particular, reluctance may also stem from a feeling that they are less responsible historically for the Palestinians' current situation than Israel, the United States, and Europe.

Source: World Bank; Palestinian Central Bureau of Statistics.

Figure 1. West Bank and Gaza Strip Gross Domestic Product (GDP) Per Capita: 1999-2009.

Conclusion

Implementing U.S. bilateral assistance programs for the West Bank and Gaza and making UNRWA contributions presents significant challenges due both to regional political uncertainty and to concerns that aid might be diverted to Palestinian terrorist groups—particularly as Congress observes how the May 2011 Fatah-Hamas power-sharing agreement might be implemented. Prospects for stability in the West Bank appear to hinge on improved security, political and economic development, Israeli cooperation, and continuation of high levels of foreign assistance.

In assessing whether U.S. aid to the Palestinians since the June 2007 West Bank/Fatah-Gaza Strip/Hamas split has advanced U.S. interests, Congress could evaluate how successful aid has been in

- reducing the threat of terrorism;
- inclining Palestinians towards peace with Israel;
- preparing Palestinians for self-reliance in security, political, and economic matters;
- promoting regional stability; and
- meeting humanitarian needs.

Given that evaluation, Congress will assess future aid in the context of U.S. policy priorities (see "Issues for Congress in Determining Future Aid" and "Introduction: Issues for Congress"). Such evaluation and assessment might influence its deliberations over

- which aid programs to start, continue, expand, scale back, change, or end; and
- which oversight, vetting, monitoring, and evaluation requirements to apply to various aid programs.

End Notes

[1] For more information on Hamas and these terrorist designations, see CRS Report R41514, *Hamas: Background and Issues for Congress*, by Jim Zanotti.

[2] Those conditions are that Hamas members of a Palestinian power-sharing government (1) recognize Israel's right to exist, (2) renounce violence, and (3) accept previous Israeli-Palestinian agreements.

[3] Prior to the establishment of limited Palestinian self-rule in the West Bank and Gaza, approximately $170 million in U.S. developmental and humanitarian assistance (not including contributions to UNRWA) were obligated for Palestinians in the West Bank and Gaza from 1975-1993, mainly through non-governmental organizations. CRS Report 93-689 F, *West Bank/Gaza Strip: U.S. Foreign Assistance*, by Clyde R. Mark, July 27, 1993, available on request to Jim Zanotti.

[4] See U.N. Development Programme 2007/08 Human Development Report, Table 18: Flows of Aid, Private Capital and Debt, available at http://hdr.undp.org/en/media

[5] For competing accounts of the events surrounding the Hamas takeover, see CRS Report R41514, *Hamas: Background and Issues for Congress*, by Jim Zanotti.

[6] Conditions, limitations, and restrictions for FY2011 are contained in the Consolidated Appropriations Act, 2010, P.L. 111-117, Secs. 7034-7040, as these provisions' application has been extended pursuant to the Department of Defense and Continuing Appropriations Act, 2011 (P.L. 112-10).

[7] Although a Hamas-majority PLC could technically pass legislation controlling various functions of the PA government, a document summarizing a May 16, 2011, 3D Security Initiative briefing for a congressional staff audience stated that the PLC would not likely play an activist role—absent widespread consensus across factions— given the interim nature of the power-sharing agreement as a placeholder anticipating PA presidential and legislative elections.

[8] P.L. 111-117, Secs. 7039-7040, 7042(f). GAO audits are available on the following U.S. aid programs to the Palestinians: (1) Economic Support Fund, including direct assistance to the PA and project assistance (audit for FY2008-FY2009 accessible at http://www.gao.gov /new.items/d10623r.pdf), (2) security assistance to the PA through the International Narcotics Control and Law Enforcement account (http://www.gao.gov/new.items

/d10505.pdf), and (3) contributions to UNRWA through the Migration and Refugee Assistance and Emergency Refugee and Migration Assistance accounts (http://www.gao. gov/new.items/d09622.pdf).

[9] For example, see the State Department's Middle East Partnership Initiative (MEPI) West Bank/Gaza website at http://mepi.state

[10] The State Department's FY2012 Congressional Budget Justification for Foreign Operations (Annex: Regional Perspectives), p. 571, available at http://www.state stated that "The United States will continue to respond to humanitarian needs in Gaza as they arise, through emergency assistance to the most vulnerable populations through nongovernmental organizations not controlled by Hamas or other foreign terrorist organizations. All assistance programs for Gaza, consistent with legislative requirements, will work through vetted local, U.S., or international nongovernmental organizations to meet U.S. objectives and follow established safeguards that will ensure funding is only used where, how, and by whom it is intended. The United States will similarly continue to work with the Government of Israel to try to develop an effective crossings protocol that improves the flow of humanitarian, recovery, and commercial goods into and out of Gaza without compromising Israel's security."

[11] For further detail on the types of projects funded, see GAO, *Foreign Assistance: U.S. Assistance to the West Bank and Gaza for Fiscal Years 2008 and 2009*, May 14, 2010, available at http://www.gao.gov/new.items/d10623r.pdf.

[12] P.L. 111-117, Sec. 7039(b) sets forth the legal requirements for vetting: "Prior to the obligation of funds appropriated by this Act under the heading 'Economic Support Fund' for assistance for the West Bank and Gaza, the Secretary of State shall take all appropriate steps to ensure that such assistance is not provided to or through any individual, private or government entity, or educational institution that the Secretary knows or has reason to believe advocates, plans, sponsors, engages in, or has engaged in, terrorist activity nor, with respect to private entities or educational institutions, those that have as a principal officer of the entity's governing board or governing board of trustees any individual that has been determined to be involved in, or advocating terrorist activity or determined to be a member of a designated foreign terrorist organization: *Provided*, That the Secretary of State shall, as appropriate, establish procedures specifying the steps to be taken in carrying out this subsection and shall terminate assistance to any individual, entity, or educational institution which the Secretary has determined to be involved in or advocating terrorist activity."

[13] "Audit: Terrorists Got U.S. Aid; Agency's Screening Called Inadequate," *Chicago Tribune*, November 16, 2007; Testimony of Henrietta Fore, USAID Administrator and Director of U.S. Foreign Assistance, House Appropriations Subcommittee on State, Foreign Operations, and Related Programs Holds Hearing on the Fiscal 2009 Budget for the U.S. Agency for International Development, February 27, 2008.

[14] Statement issued by USAID to CRS on February 5, 2009. USAID does not subject U.S. organizations to vetting due to U.S. privacy law concerns. See GAO, *Measures to Prevent Inadvertent Payments to Terrorists Under Palestinian* Aid Programs Have Been Strengthened, but Some Weaknesses Remain, GAO Foreign Assistance Report 09-622, May 2009, available at http://www.gao.gov/new.items/d09622.pdf.

[15] See GAO, Measures to Prevent Inadvertent Payments to Terrorists..., op. cit. A schematic detailing USAID's vetting process is found on page 42 of the report. GAO did recommend in the report that USAID take steps to ensure that it and its primary contractors use the same rigor at the subcontractor level that they employed in requiring antiterrorism clauses and certifications during their contracting process.

[16] Ileana Ros-Lehtinen, Chairwoman of the House Foreign Affairs Committee, voiced significant concern over the Administration's provision of direct budgetary assistance to the PA when serving as Ranking Member in November 2010: "It is deeply disturbing that the Administration is continuing to bail out the Palestinian leadership when they continue to fail to meet their commitments, under international agreements and requirements outlined in U.S. law, including dismantling the Palestinian terrorist infrastructure, combating corruption, stopping anti-Israel and anti-Semitic incitement, and recognizing Israel's right to exist as a Jewish state." House Foreign Affairs Committee website: "Ros-Lehtinen Opposes Latest U.S. 'Bailout' Installment for Palestinian Authority," November 11, 2010, available at http://republicans.foreignaffairs.house.gov/press_display.asp?id=1630.

[17] See P.L. 111-117, Sec. 7040 ("Limitation on Assistance for the Palestinian Authority"). In the event of a presidential waiver, Sec. 7040 requires the President to submit a report to the Committees on Appropriations "detailing the justification for the waiver, the purposes for which the funds will be spent, and the accounting procedures in place to ensure that the funds are properly disbursed. The report shall also detail the steps the Palestinian Authority has taken to arrest terrorists, confiscate weapons and dismantle the terrorist infrastructure."

[18] Congressional briefing with State Department and USAID officials, July 9, 2009.

[19] Presidential Determination No. 2009-23.

[20] Presidential Memorandum 2010-06, available at http://www.whitehouse.gov/the-press-office/presidentialdetermination-waiver

[21] Presidential Determination 2011-1, available at http://www.whitehouse.gov/the-press-office/2010/10/07/presidentialmemorandum-providing-funds

[22] USAID, FY2011 Congressional Notification #1, October 7, 2010.

[23] For further information on this subject, see CRS Report R40664, *U.S. Security Assistance to the Palestinian Authority*, by Jim Zanotti.

[24] See, e.g., Ian Cobain, "CIA working with Palestinian security agents," *guardian*, December 17, 2009; Yezid Sayigh, "'Fixing Broken Windows': Security Sector Reform in Palestine, Lebanon and Yemen," Carnegie Endowment for International Peace, October 2009, available at http://www.carnegieendowment.org/files/security_sector_reform

[25] See, e.g., Nathan Thrall, "Our Man in Palestine," *New York Review of Books*, October 14, 2010, available at http://www.nybooks.com/articles/archives/2010/oct/14/our-man. For further discussion of human rights concerns surrounding PA security forces in the West Bank and Hamas in Gaza, see CRS Report R40664, *U.S. Security Assistance to the Palestinian Authority*, by Jim Zanotti; Human Rights Watch, *Internal Fight: Palestinian Abuses in Gaza and the West Bank*, July 29, 2008, available at http://www.hrw.org/en/reports/2008/07/29/internal-fight-0.

[26] See International Crisis Group, *Squaring the Circle: Palestinian Security Reform Under Occupation*, Middle East Report No. 98, September 7, 2010, available at http://www.crisisgroup.org/~/media 0the%20Circle%20--%20Palestinian%20Security%20Reform %20under%20Occupation.ashx; International Crisis Group, *Ruling Palestine II: The West Bank Model?* Middle East Report No. 79, July 17, 2008, available at http://www.crisisgroup.org/library/documents/middle_east___north_africa/arab_israeli_conflict ___the_west_bank_model.pdf. These operations underscore the fact that the Israeli-Palestinian agreements that authorized the creation of Palestinian security forces in the 1990s in areas of limited Palestinian self-rule contained clauses that preserved Israel's prerogative to conduct operations in those areas for purposes of its own security.

[27] According to UNRWA's website

(http://www.unrwa.org/userfiles/file/financial U.S. contributions in 2009 constituted approximately 20% of the UNRWA General Fund budget and 27% of the total budget. Aggregate contributions from the European Commission and European states (including both EU members and non-members) and regions constituted approximately 52% of the total budget.

[28] See, e.g., Michael S. Bernstam, "The Palestinian Proletariat," *Commentary*, December 2010.

[29] See FY2011 Congressional Budget Justification for Foreign Operations, Department of State (Volume 2), p. 86, available at http://www.state "U.S. government support for UNRWA directly contributes to the U.S. strategic interest of meeting the humanitarian needs of Palestinians, while promoting their self-sufficiency. UNRWA plays a stabilizing role in the Middle East through its assistance programs, serving as an important counterweight to extremist elements."

[30] See James G. Lindsay, *Fixing UNRWA: Repairing the UN's Troubled System of Aid to Palestinian Refugees*, Washington Institute of Near East Policy Policy Focus #91, January 2009, available at http://www.thewashingtoninstitute.org/pubPDFs/PolicyFocus91.pdf. See also James Phillips, "The Gaza Aid Package: Time to Rethink U.S. Foreign Assistance to the Palestinians," The Heritage Foundation WebMemo No. 2333, March 9, 2009, available at http://www.heritage.org/Research/MiddleEast/wm2333.cfm.

[31] A direct written rebuttal by Israeli academic Maya Rosenfeld to the former UNRWA general counsel's critiques was carried by UNRWA's website and is available at http://rete-eco.it/attachments/5172_Rejoinder%20to%20Lindsay_jan09.pdf.

[32] Transcript of remarks by Secretary of State Hillary Rodham Clinton, House Appropriations Subcommittee on State, Foreign Operations and Related Programs hearing: "Supplemental Request," April 23, 2009.

[33] GAO, *Measures to Prevent Inadvertent Payments to Terrorists...*, op. cit.

[34] Ibid.

[35] Ibid.

[36] "Framework for Cooperation Between UNRWA and the Government of the United States of America for 2011," available at http://www.state. The 15 enumerated criteria are found in Annex 4 of the framework document.

[37] GAO, *Measures to Prevent Inadvertent Payments to Terrorists...*, op. cit. In 2006, an organization that advocates for Palestinian refugees estimated the total number of 1967 displaced persons to be between 800,000 and 850,000. See BADIL Resource Center for Palestinian Residency & Refugee Rights, *Survey of Palestinian Refugees and Internally Displaced Persons 2004-2005*, May 2006, available at http://www.badil.org/en/documents/category/35-publications?download=135%3Asurvey04-05.

[38] GAO, *Measures to Prevent Inadvertent Payments to Terrorists...*, op. cit.

[39] U.S. General Services Administration website at https://www.acquisition.gov/faqs_whatis.asp.

[40] CRS correspondence with State Department, August 9, 2010.

[41] GAO, *Measures to Prevent Inadvertent Payments to Terrorists...*, op. cit.

[42] Ibid.

[43] CRS correspondence with State Department, August 2010.

[44] Ibid.

[45] U.S. Citizenship and Immigration Services bureau website at http://www.uscis.gov/portal/site/uscis/menuitem.5af9bb95919f35e66f614176543f6d1a/?vgnextoid=e4eabcf527f93210 VgnVCM100000b92ca60aRCRD&vgnextchannel= 385d3e4d77d73210VgnVCM100000082ca60aRCRD.

[46] CRS correspondence with State Department, July 2009.

[47] CRS correspondence with State Department, August 2010.

[48] Ibid.

[49] See H.Rept. 111-151, Joint Explanatory Statement of the Committee of Conference, Title XI, "Migration and Refugee Assistance." Also during the 111th Congress, Representative Ileana Ros-Lehtinen, the Ranking Minority Member on the House Committee for Foreign Affairs, sponsored H.R. 557 (United Nations Transparency, Accountability, and Reform Act of 2009), which included a section entitled "Withholding of United States Contributions to UNRWA," with over 100 co-sponsors; and Representative Steven Rothman sponsored H.Con.Res. 29 ("Expressing the sense of Congress that the United Nations should take immediate steps to improve the transparency and accountability of the United Nations Relief and Works Agency for Palestinian Refugees (UNRWA) in the Near East to ensure that it is not providing funding, employment, or other support to terrorists") with over 30 co-sponsors. Both H.R. 557 and H.Con.Res. 29 were referred to the House Committee on Foreign Affairs in January 2009. Ranking Member Ros-Lehtinen subsequently introduced H.R. 5065 (UNRWA Humanitarian Accountability Act) with over 25 co-sponsors. H.R. 5065 is nearly identical to the section pertaining to UNRWA found in H.R. 557, and was referred to the House Committee on Foreign Affairs in April 2010.

[50] Both proposed resolutions' ninth "resolved" clauses support "the position taken by Secretary of State Hillary Clinton on April 22, 2009, that the United States 'will not deal with or in any way fund a Palestinian government that includes Hamas unless and until Hamas has renounced violence, recognized Israel and agreed to follow the previous obligations of the Palestinian Authority'".

[51] Transcript of House Appropriations Subcommittee on State, Foreign Operations and Related Programs hearing: "Supplemental Request," April 23, 2009. In the four years since the 2006 war between Israel and Hezbollah, the United States has provided robust levels of both economic and security assistance to Lebanon to (1) help with post-conflict reconstruction and to win "hearts and minds" of Lebanese citizens and (2) strengthen the Lebanese military to adequately patrol Lebanon's porous borders with Syria and prevent Hezbollah's rearmament. See CRS Report R40054, *Lebanon: Background and U.S. Relations*, by Casey L. Addis.

[52] On the previous occasions in which Hamas participated in the PA government from 2006-2007, the European Union joined the United States in refusing to provide direct assistance to the PA. There are indications, however, that Europeans might be less willing to follow the U.S. lead in the event that another PA government including Hamas is formed. See Muriel Asseburg and Paul Salem, "No Euro-Mediterranean Community without peace," EU Institute for Security Studies and European Institute of the Mediterranean, September 2009, available at http://www.iss.europa.eu/uploads/media Andrew Rettman, "EU Countries Practice 'Secret' Diplomacy, Hamas Says," *euobserver.com*, September 14, 2009.

[53] See Transcript of translated remarks (from Hebrew) by Prime Minister Binyamin Netanyahu, Tel Aviv, Israel, June 14, 2009, available at http://www.pmo.gov.il/PMOEng/Communication/PMSpeaks/speechbarilan140609.htm.

[54] For further discussion of this issue, see CRS Report R40092, *Israel and the Palestinians: Prospects for a Two-State Solution*, by Jim Zanotti.

[55] The eighth "resolved" clause in H.Res. 268 "affirms that Palestinian efforts to circumvent direct negotiations and pursue recognition of statehood prior to agreement with Israel will harm United States-Palestinian relations and will have serious implications for the United States assistance programs for the Palestinians and the Palestinians [sic] Authority". The

eighth "resolved" clause in S.Res. 185 reads that the Senate would "consider restrictions on aid to the Palestinian Authority should it persist in efforts to circumvent direct negotiations by turning to the United Nations or other international bodies".

56 A December 2010 *Washington Post* article described the situation in Gaza with respect to issues such as (1) the limited operation of conveyor belts and passage of supply trucks at crossings, (2) concerns about sewage contamination and drinking water shortages, and (3) comparisons between construction materials available through the crossings for internationally-supervised projects and those smuggled into Gaza through tunnels from Egypt for Hamas-led construction projects. Janine Zacharia, "Aid groups decry Israel's Gaza constraints," *Washington Post,* December 21, 2010. See, also, e.g., Amnesty International UK, et al., "Dashed Hopes: Continuation of the Gaza Blockade," November 30, 2010, available at http://www.oxfam.org/sites/www.oxfam.org/files/dashed-hopes-continuation-gazablockade-301110-en.pdf; Sarah A. Topol, "'Gaza Is Not Darfur!'", *Slate.com,* August 5, 2010.

57 See footnote 10. The December 2010 *Washington Post* article said that UNRWA has built 151 housing units out of the 10,000 it hopes to build, and has only received Israeli approval to build six out of the 100 schools UNRWA says are needed to accommodate 40,000 children, while Hamas claims that it has renovated 1,000 houses and built a school with materials smuggled into Gaza through the help of Islamic charities from the Gulf region. Zacharia, op. cit.

58 Text of Letter to the President, January 20, 2010, available at http://docs.google 0%2FGaza_letter_to_Obama.pdf.

59 See Sherifa Zuhur, Ali Abunimah, Haim Malka, Shibley Telhami, "Symposium: Hamas and the Two-State Solution: Villain, Victim or Missing Ingredient?" *Middle East Policy,* vol. 15, issue 2, July 1, 2008; Transcript of National Public Radio interview ("All Things Considered") with Robert Malley, June 16, 2007, available at http://www.npr.org/templates/story/story.php?storyId=11135538.

60 See Nathan J. Brown, "Fayyad Is Not the Problem, but Fayyadism Is Not the Solution to Palestine's Political Crisis," Carnegie Endowment for International Peace, September 2010, http://www.carnegieendowment.org/files/fayyad_not_problem_2.pdf.

61 See, e.g., Palestinian National Authority, *Palestine: Ending the Occupation, Establishing the State,* Program of the Thirteenth Government, August 2009, available at http://www.mideastweb.org/palestine_state. A key passage from the document reads: "Out of respect for our citizens, and in recognition of their desire to live free and peaceful lives under national independence, we must answer their demand to see the fruits of the state-building project. Against this background, the Palestinian government is struggling determinedly against a hostile occupation regime, employing all of its energies and available resources, most especially the capacities of our people, to complete the process of building institutions of the independent State of Palestine in order to establish a de facto state apparatus within the next two years. It is time now for the illegal occupation to end and for the Palestinian people to enjoy security, safety, freedom and independence."

62 The current system of Israeli restrictions on movement within the West Bank can be traced to the time of the second Palestinian *intifada* (which began in late 2000), and the closure of Gaza crossings and ports following the Hamas takeover in June 2007 has led to a near economic standstill there. The International Crisis Group has referred to a UNDP official's estimate that it would take five years for Gaza to be restored simply to the unenviable state in which it was immediately before the recent conflict began in December 2008.

International Crisis Group, *Gaza's Unfinished Business*, Middle East Report No. 85, April 23, 2009, available at http://www.crisisgroup.org/~/media nfinished%20Business.ashx.

[63] Zones denoted as "Area C" in the West Bank pursuant to the Israel-PLO Interim Agreement on the West Bank and the Gaza Strip, dated September 28, 1995, fall under Israeli administrative and security control. The agreement is available at http://www.mfa.gov.il/MFA/Peace+Process/Guide+to+the+Peace+Process/THE+ISRAELI-PALESTINIAN+INTERIM+AGREEMENT.htm.

[64] See Nathan J. Brown, "Are Palestinians Building a State?", Carnegie Endowment for International Peace, June 2010, available at http://www.carnegieendowment.org/files/palestinian_state1.pdf.

[65] Some of these ventures have been supported by U.S. organizations—including the Overseas Private Investment Corporation (OPIC), the Aspen Institute, the Center for American Progress, and CHF International—affiliated or involved with a public-private partnership known as the Middle East Investment Initiative. See http://meiinitiative.org.

[66] The World Bank, Statement at the Ad Hoc Liaison Committee Meeting, Brussels, Belgium, April 13, 2011, available at http://siteresources.worldbank.org/WESTBANKGAZAEXTN/Resources/AHLCApril2011WorldBankStatement.pdf.

[67] See The World Bank, op. cit.; Zahi Khouri, "The West Bank's Deceptive Growth," *New York Times*, September 8, 2009.

[68] See, e.g., H.Rept. 111-366: "The conferees direct the Secretary of State to provide a report to the Committees on Appropriations not later than 180 days after enactment of this Act on international participation, including by Arab states, in the economic development of the West Bank and support for the Palestinian Authority, similar to that proposed by the House. This report may be submitted in classified form, if necessary."

[69] See Glenn Kessler, "Arab Aid to Palestinians Often Doesn't Fulfill Pledges," *Washington Post*, July 27, 2008; "Falling Short," *Washington Post*, July 27, 2008, available at http://www.washingtonpost.com/wp-dyn/content/graphic/2008/07/27/GR2008072700095.html?sid=ST2008072700226.

In: United States Assistance for the Palestinians ISBN: 978-1-62100-830-9
Editors: J. M. Bailey and P. F. Miller

Chapter 2

PALESTINIAN AUTHORITY: UNITED STATES ASSISTANCE IS TRAINING AND EQUIPPING SECURITY FORCES, BUT THE PROGRAM NEEDS TO MEASURE PROGRESS AND FACES LOGISTICAL CONSTRAINTS*

United States Government Accountability Office

WHY GAO DID THIS STUDY

The 2003 Roadmap for Peace process sponsored by the United States and other nations obligates the Palestinian Authority (PA) and the Government of Israel to undertake security efforts as a necessary precursor for achieving the long-standing objective of establishing a Palestinian state as part of the two-state solution for peace in the Middle East. In 2005 the Department of State (State) created the office of the United States Security Coordinator (USSC) to help the parties meet these obligations.

GAO was asked to (1) describe the nature and extent of U.S. security assistance to the PA since 2007; (2) assess State's efforts to measure the

* This is an edited, reformatted and augmented version of a United States Government Accountability Office publication, Report to the Committee on Foreign Affairs and Its Subcommittee on the Middle East and South Asia, House of Representatives, GAO-10-505, dated May 2010.

effectiveness of its security assistance; and (3) describe factors that may affect the implementation of U.S. security assistance programs. GAO analyzed documents; interviewed officials and regional experts; and conducted fieldwork in Jerusalem, the West Bank, Israel, and Jordan.

What GAO Recommends

GAO recommends that, as State develops the USSC campaign plan for providing security assistance to the PA, the Secretary of State should define specific objectives and establish outcome-based indicators enabling it to assess progress.

State partially concurred with this recommendation. It agreed with the need for more performance-based indicators, but noted that factors outside its control influence progress.

What GAO Found

State has allocated about $392 million to train and equip the PA security forces, oversee construction of related infrastructure projects, and develop the capacity of the PA during fiscal years 2007 through 2010. Of this total, State has allocated: (1) more than $160 million to help fund and support training, primarily for the PA's National Security Force (NSF); (2) approximately $89 million to provide nonlethal equipment; (3) about $99 million to renovate or construct several PA installations, including two of the operations camps it plans to provide (see figure); and (4) about $22 million to build the capacity of the Interior Ministry and its Strategic Planning Directorate. State also requested $150 million for its programs for fiscal year 2011.

Although U.S. and international officials said that U.S. security assistance programs for the PA have helped to improve security conditions in some West Bank areas, State and USSC have not established clear and measurable outcome-based performance indicators to assess progress. Thus, it is difficult to determine how the programs support the achievement of security-related Roadmap obligations. U.S. officials attributed the lack of agreement on such performance indicators to a number of factors, including the relatively early stage of PA plans and capacity for reforming, rebuilding, and sustaining its security forces. Developing outcome-based indicators to measure and manage performance against program goals has been identified by GAO as a good management practice. Such indicators would help USSC provide objective and useful performance information for decision makers. State and USSC officials noted that they plan to incorporate performance indicators in a USSC campaign plan to be released in mid-2010.

The implementation of the U.S. security assistance programs faces logistical constraints largely outside of U.S. control, and these implementation efforts outpace international efforts to develop the limited capacity of the PA police and justice sector. Logistical constraints include restrictions on the movement of USSC personnel in the West Bank, lack of a process to ensure approval and timely delivery of equipment, and difficulties in acquiring suitable land for infrastructure projects. State, USAID, and other international donors have been assisting the PA civil police and justice-sector reforms, although these efforts are not proceeding at the same pace as the security assistance programs.

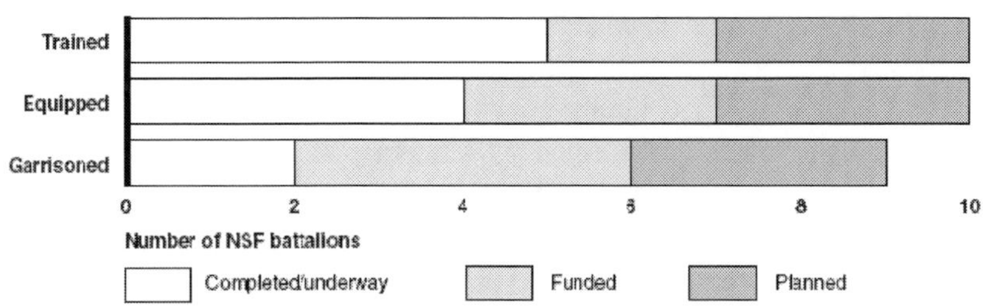

Figure 1. Status of USSC Security Assistance to the PA as of March 2010.

ABBREVIATIONS

ATA	Anti Terrorism Assistance Program (State Bureau of Diplomatic Security)
BST	British Support Team
DOD	U.S. Department of Defense
ESF	Economic Support Funds
EUPOL COPPS	European Union Police Coordination Office for Palestinian Police Support
GPRA	Government Performance and Results Act
INCLE	International Narcotics Control and Law Enforcement

INL	Bureau of International Narcotics and Law Enforcement Affairs
JIPTC	Jordan International Police Training Center
JSAP	Justice Sector Assistance Project
MTT	Mobile Training Team
NSF	National Security Forces
OCHA	United Nations Office for the Coordination of Humanitarian Affairs
PA	Palestinian Authority
PASF	Palestinian Authority Security Forces
PCP	Palestinian Civil Police
PG	Presidential Guard
PLO	Palestine Liberation Organization
PRDP	Palestinian Reform and Development Plan
SLC	Senior Leaders Course
SPD	Strategic Planning Directorate
SPF	Special Police Force
SSWG	Security Sector Working Group
UN	United Nations
USAID	U.S. Agency for International Development
USSC	U.S. Security Coordinator

May 11, 2010

The Honorable Howard L. Berman Chairman
The Honorable Ileana Ros-Lehtinen Ranking Member
Committee on Foreign Affairs
House of Representatives

The Honorable Gary L. Ackerman Chairman
The Honorable Dan Burton
Ranking Member
Subcommittee on the Middle East and South Asia
Committee on Foreign Affairs House of Representatives

Since 1993, the U.S. government has committed more than $3.5 billion in bilateral aid to the Palestinians, providing humanitarian, development, and security assistance for the West Bank and Gaza. In 2002, the United States outlined the principles for a performance-based strategy for settling the Israeli-Palestinian conflict. This strategy— known informally as the Roadmap for Peace (Roadmap)—calls for an independent Palestinian state coexisting peacefully with the State of Israel and, among other things, presents a plan for establishing the security preconditions necessary for such a state.[1] The United Nations, the United States, the European Union, and Russia—known as the Quartet on the Middle East[2]— as well as Israel and the Palestinian Authority (PA) endorsed the strategy in April 2003. To help the PA and Israel meet their Roadmap obligations and pave the way for a two-state solution, the Secretary of State created the Jerusalem-based office of the United States Security Coordinator (USSC) in 2005 to facilitate PA-Israeli cooperation and coordinate assistance for the Palestinian Authority Security Forces (PASF) provided by the United States and other international donors. Beginning in 2007, USSC and the State Department's (State) Bureau of International Narcotics and Law Enforcement Affairs (INL) have funded and helped train, equip, and house PA security personnel based in the West Bank.

In this report, we (1) describe the nature and extent of U.S. security assistance to the Palestinian Authority since 2007; (2) assess State's efforts to measure the effectiveness of its security assistance; and (3) describe factors that may affect the implementation of U.S. security assistance programs.

To address these objectives, we reviewed relevant documents and interviewed officials from State, the Department of Defense (DOD), and the U.S. Agency for International Development (USAID) in Washington, D.C., and in Israel, Jerusalem, Jordan, and the West Bank. We met with PA and Israeli government officials as well as recognized experts in Israeli-Palestinian affairs. To describe the nature and extent of U.S. security assistance, we also conducted site visits to observe U.S.-sponsored training and construction projects. To assess State's efforts to measure the effectiveness of its security assistance programs, we examined whether State's approach identified and applied measurable outcome-based performance indicators to measure and manage performance against its results-oriented goals, which GAO has identified as a good management practice because it helps provide objective and useful performance information for decision makers when faced with limited resources and competing priorities.[3]

We conducted our work from July 2009 to May 2010 and in accordance with generally accepted government auditing standards. Those standards require that we plan and perform the audit to obtain sufficient, appropriate evidence to provide a reasonable basis for our findings and conclusions based on our audit objectives. We believe that the evidence obtained provides a reasonable basis for our findings and conclusions based on our audit objectives. See appendix I for more detailed information about our scope and methodology.

RESULTS IN BRIEF

State has allocated a total of approximately $392 million to train and equip the PASF, oversee construction of related infrastructure projects, and develop the capacity of the PA during fiscal years 2007 through 2010. State, through the USSC, has allocated more than $160 million of the total to help fund the training of PASF units. As of January 2010, one Presidential Guard battalion and four National Security Forces (NSF) special battalions had received basic training in Jordan, and State plans to help fund training for six additional NSF special battalions beginning in 2010.[4] Moreover, USSC has conducted or supported about 24 different specialized courses for PASF personnel in the West Bank since mid-2008. In addition, State has allocated almost $89 million of the total to provide the NSF and Presidential Guard with vehicles and nonlethal equipment, including uniforms with protective gear; operational equipment such as riot shields, batons, and hand cuffs; computers; tents; and basic first aid kits. The USSC expects to issue each battalion trained in Jordan an initial allotment of this equipment. As of March 2010, one battalion had received its full issuance of equipment, and four more were in the process of being equipped. State also has allocated approximately $99 million of the total to fund and oversee the renovation or construction of several PASF installations, including two training centers and two operations camps. In addition, USSC and the PA plan to build seven more operations camps to house battalions that receive U.S.-sponsored training.[5] Finally, State has allocated approximately $22 million of the total to build the capacity of the Ministry of the Interior, focusing on the creation of the Strategic Planning Directorate, a small group responsible for conducting longer-term strategic planning for the Ministry and the PASF.[6] State also has requested a total of $150 million in additional funding for security assistance to the PA for fiscal year 2011 to continue these activities, including $56 million for training, $33 million for equipment, $53 million for infrastructure, and $3 million for strategic capacity building activities.

Although U.S. and international officials said that U.S. security assistance has helped the PA improve security conditions in some areas of the West

Bank, State and USSC have not established clear and measurable outcome-based performance indicators for assessing the progress of their security assistance programs for the PA. We have previously identified the development of such indicators as a good management practice because it helps provide objective and useful performance information for executive decision makers and overseers. State documents and annual mission strategic plans for the U.S. Consulate General in Jerusalem identify performance indicators for U.S. security assistance programs; however, the targets they set to measure progress toward these indicators focus on specific program outputs, such as the number of battalions or personnel trained and equipped, rather than on broader program outcomes such as helping the PA meet its Roadmap obligations to achieve the transformation of its security sector and create a professional, right-sized PASF.[7] U.S. officials attributed the lack of agreement on clear and measurable outcome-based performance indicators to a number of factors. For example, the PA plans and capacity for reforming, rebuilding, and sustaining its security forces are changeable and still in a relatively early stage of development, making it difficult for the PA to set targets that the USSC could use to measure the progress and effectiveness of its programs. Nevertheless, State and USSC officials noted that they plan to incorporate such performance indicators to the extent possible in a USSC campaign plan being developed for release in mid-2010.

The implementation of the U.S. security assistance programs faces a number of logistical constraints that are largely outside of U.S. control, and these security assistance programs outpace efforts to develop the limited capacity of the PA police and justice sector. Logistical constraints include restrictions on the movement and access of USSC personnel in the West Bank, a lack of a process to ensure approval and timely delivery of equipment shipments, and difficulties in acquiring suitable land for infrastructure projects in the relatively small portion of the West Bank in which the PASF is allowed to construct or maintain facilities. For example, State and USSC officials noted that the process for obtaining Government of Israel approval for the shipment and delivery of equipment for the PASF is lengthy and may hamper the timely arrival of U.S. shipments. Moreover, the USSC lacks the means to hold the Government of Israel or the PA accountable if shipments are delayed or approvals withheld.[8] Furthermore, U.S. and PA officials said sustaining the progress they have made with U.S. assistance in the security sector may be difficult due to the lack of capacity in the civil police and the justice sectors with which the USSC-supported security forces must operate. State, USAID, and other international donors have been assisting the PA with civil police and justice-sector reforms, although these programs are not proceeding at the same pace as the programs to train and equip the security forces and build the capacity of the Ministry of the Interior.

As State develops the USSC campaign plan for providing security assistance to the PA, we recommend that the Secretary of State establish outcome-based indicators and track them over time. State should define specific program objectives and identify appropriate outcome-based indicators that would demonstrate progress toward achieving those objectives, and would enable it to, among other things, weigh the progress made in developing the security forces, civil police, Ministry of Interior, and justice sector.

State provided written comments on a draft of this report, which are reprinted in appendix IV. State partially concurred with our recommendation, agreeing that more performance-based indicators are needed. Consistent with our report, State also cited that several factors outside of their control influence progress toward a number of meaningful performance-based indicators.

BACKGROUND

The Palestinian territories, comprising the West Bank and Gaza, cover 2,402 square miles and have a combined population of over 4 million people.[9] (See fig. 2.) Both the PA and Israel administer areas within the West Bank.

Security Assistance to PA Since 1993

The U.S. government, along with other countries, has provided intermittent security assistance to the Palestinians since 1993.

1993-2003

In 1993, the Oslo Accord called for limited Palestinian self-rule and security responsibilities in the West Bank and Gaza.[10] The subsequent 1995 Interim Agreement on the West Bank and the Gaza Strip divided the West Bank into three zones and allotted civil and security responsibilities, to varying degrees, to the Israeli government and the PA. The Government of Israel allowed the PA to establish some security forces and coordinated with the PA on the establishment of limited self-rule in the West Bank and Gaza. The United States provided some non-lethal equipment and a small amount of funding for salaries to help the newly created PA security forces improve their professionalism and combat terrorism. Other countries provided the PA with security assistance focused on training and equipping the security forces.

Sources: GAO (data); CIA and Map Resources (map).

Figure 2. Map of West Bank and Gaza and Surrounding Countries.

The outbreak of the second intifada (insurrection), which State reports resulted in the death of more than 3,000 Palestinians and about 1,000 Israelis between 2000 and 2004, disrupted security assistance efforts.[11] In response to the intifada, the Israeli security forces reoccupied much of the West Bank previously ceded to PA control, set up hundreds of checkpoints and roadblocks throughout the territory, erected a wall separating Israel and some Palestinian territory from the rest of the West Bank, and destroyed much of the Palestinian security infrastructure. As a result, Israeli-Palestinian security cooperation ceased and other governments curtailed or halted their security assistance to the PA. Amid the violence, efforts to negotiate a Middle East peace agreement began in 2000 at Camp David and continued until 2003.

2003-2007

Security assistance efforts did not resume until after the PA, Israel, United States, United Nations, European Union, and Russia agreed in 2003 to implement the Roadmap for Peace, a U.S.-proposed performance-based strategy, which calls for an independent Palestinian state coexisting peacefully with the State of Israel and, among other things, provides a plan for establishing the security preconditions necessary to create an independent Palestinian state. The Roadmap, among other things, obligates the PA and Israel to undertake specific actions to improve security as part of the ongoing Middle East peace process. In particular, the Roadmap obligates the PA to perform the following actions:

- Issue an unequivocal statement reiterating Israel's right to exist in peace and security and calling for an immediate and unconditional ceasefire to end armed activity and all acts of violence against Israelis anywhere. All official Palestinian institutions end incitement against Israel.
- Have its rebuilt and refocused security apparatus begin sustained, targeted, and effective operations aimed at confronting all those engaged in terror and dismantlement of terrorist capabilities and infrastructure. This includes commencing confiscation of illegal weapons and consolidation of security authority, free of association with terror and corruption.
- Consolidate all Palestinian security organizations into three services reporting to an empowered Interior Minister.

In return, the Roadmap obligates the Israelis to perform the following actions:

- Issue an unequivocal statement affirming its commitment to the two-state vision of an independent, viable, sovereign Palestinian state living in peace and security alongside Israel, as expressed by President Bush, and calling for an immediate end to violence against Palestinians everywhere. All official Israeli institutions are also to end incitement against Palestinians.
- Take no actions undermining trust, including deportations, attacks on civilians; confiscation and/or demolition of Palestinian homes and property, as a punitive measure or to facilitate Israeli construction; destruction of Palestinian institutions and infrastructure; and other measures specified in the Tenet work plan;[12] and
- Progressively withdraw the Israeli Defense Forces from areas occupied since September 28, 2000, and the two sides restore the status quo that existed prior to September 28, 2000, as comprehensive security performance moves forward. Palestinian security forces to progressively redeploy to areas vacated by the Israeli Defense Forces.

To help the PA and Israel meet their Roadmap obligations and pave the way for a two-state solution, the Secretary of State created the office of the USSC in 2005. The USSC, which operated with no project funding until mid-2007, initially focused on providing advice and guidance to the PASF on its reform efforts while also coordinating the programs of several other security donors. In addition, USSC officials coordinated and consulted with Israeli and Palestinian authorities in connection with the PA's assumption of responsibility for security in Gaza following Israel's August 2005 withdrawal.

In January 2006, the Palestinian people elected a Hamas majority to the Palestinian Legislative Council.[13] Following the results of the January 2006 election and the subsequent formation of a Fatah-Hamas unity government in 2007, the Quartet on the Middle East announced it would continue to provide support and assistance to the Hamas-led government only if the government would agree to nonviolence, recognize the State of Israel, and respect previous Israeli-Palestinian peace agreements.[14] Hamas never accepted these conditions. U.S. direct assistance to the Palestinians was reduced and restructured, with the focus shifting to providing humanitarian and project assistance indirectly through international and nongovernmental organizations. During this time, USSC focused on coordinating international assistance aimed at improving Gaza's economy and helped coordinate the efforts of Israel, Egypt, and the PA to regulate and control the key Gaza border crossings. USSC also coordinated with Britain and Canada to provide training assistance to the PA's Presidential Guard, a security organization under the control of the PA president with responsibility for protecting PA officials and facilities and manning the border crossings.

2007-2010

In June 2007, Hamas forcibly took control of the Gaza Strip. This led the PA President to issue an emergency decree suspending the operation of the PA government and appointing a new government, without Hamas participation, to administer the affairs of the West Bank during the state of emergency, under a politically independent Prime Minister. As a result, the United States decided to re-engage with the PA directly and increased the amount of U.S. assistance aimed at improving the economic and security climate in the West Bank and increasing the capacity of the PA.

As described by USSC and State officials, the USSC's current mission is to

1) facilitate PA-Israeli cooperation and allay Israeli fears about the nature and capabilities of the PASF;
2) lead and coordinate international assistance for the PASF provided by the United States and other international donors to eliminate duplication of effort;[15] and
3) help the PA rightsize, reform, and professionalize its security sector by advising the PA and by training and equipping the PASF to meet the Palestinians' obligations outlined in the Roadmap.

The head of the USSC, a lieutenant general in the U.S. Army, also serves as the deputy for security issues to the U.S. Special Envoy for Middle East Peace.[16]

The office of the USSC has a core staff of approximately 45 personnel as of March 2010. Headquartered in Jerusalem, the USSC includes up to 16 U.S. military personnel and several U.S. civilians. About 17 military staff provided to USSC by Canada operate in the West Bank, and two or more British military personnel from Britain support the USSC at the PA Ministry of Interior in Ramallah.[17] USSC also maintains staff at the U.S. Embassy in Tel Aviv as liaisons to the government of Israel. State's Bureau of International Narcotics and Law Enforcement Affairs (INL) maintains staff in Jerusalem to implement INL program funds, most of which underwrite USSC activities. About 28 INL-directed Dyncorps International contractors assist with USSC training programs in the West Bank and Jordan. Other INL staff and contractors manage equipment warehouse operations in Jerusalem and oversee construction projects in the West Bank under this program.

PASF

Under the current president and prime minister, the PA formalized plans to reorganize and rebuild ministries and security forces in the West Bank with donor assistance between 2008 and 2010. The PA has consolidated a 23,000-strong security force under Presidential and Interior Ministry control, as called for in the Roadmap Agreement.[18] As shown in figure 2, the PASF is comprised of uniformed services, civilian organizations, and intelligence offices.[19]

U.S. SECURITY ASSISTANCE TO THE PA EMPHASIZES TRAINING, EQUIPMENT, AND INFRASTRUCTURE AND ALSO SUPPORTS CAPACITY BUILDING

The U.S. government, through USSC and INL has allocated over $160 million in funding for the training of certain units of the PASF's uniformed services, primarily the NSF, since 2007. USSC has also helped provide State-funded vehicles and nonlethal individual and unit equipment to both the NSF and Presidential Guard, totaling about $89 million. In addition, State has allocated approximately $99 million toward the renovation or construction of numerous PASF installations. Finally, USSC and INL have undertaken activities to increase the PA's capacity, including building the Ministry of Interior's capacity to plan and oversee the PASF and coordinate international donor assistance. State allocated $22 million in funding for these programs since 2007. (See table 1.)

State also has requested a total of $150 million in additional INCLE funding for security assistance to the PA for fiscal year 2011, including $56 million for training activities, $33 million for equipping, $53 million for infrastructure activities, and $3 million for strategic capacity building activities.

Table 1. Overview of the PASF

	Service	Responsibilities	Reports to	Direct recipientof USSC assistance
Uniformed Services	National Security Forces (NSF)	A lightly armed and equipped gendarmerie-style force charged with supporting the civil police; delivering law and order; and combating terrorism, short of acting as a true military force.[a] To include 10 special battalions, with approximately 500 troops each.	Minister of Interior	Yes
	Presidential Guard	Elite force of about 2,300 personnel organized into 4 battalions, each specialized in different functions, including protection of important PA officials and facilities, quick reaction, and some gendarmerie tasks.	PA President	Yes
Civilian Security Organizations	Palestinian Civil Police	Approximately 7,300 officers responsible for daily policing, including arresting criminals, controlling traffic, and keeping general order. A relatively small, special rapid deployment unit handles complex situations such as riots or counterterrorism activities.	Minister of Interior	No
	Palestinian Civil Defense	About 650 personnel responsible for common protection services, such as emergency rescue and fire department services.	Minister of Interior	Yes
Intelligence Agencies	General Intelligence Service	Responsible for collecting intelligence inside and outside the territories, conducting counterespionage, and serving as the Palestinian liaison with other governments' intelligence agencies.	PA President	No
	Preventive Security Organization	Responsible for conducting counterterrorism efforts, monitoring opposition groups, and conducting reconnaissance and intelligence operations.	Minister of Interior	No
	Military Intelligence	Responsible for arresting and interrogating opposition activists considered a threat to the PA.	National Security Forces	No

Source: GAO analysis.

[a] Gendarmeries are specialized units of police with military skills to handle temporary hostile situations such as unruly crowds. According to a State document, the NSF serves as a "gendarme-like" organization and a back-up for the Palestinian civil police if the latter encounter overwhelming forces with heavier weapons than the police possess. The NSF is expected to function in small unit or company-size formations, in a military fashion, to support civil police to subdue civil disorders and address situations in which police Special Weapons and Tactics teams would ordinarily be used in the United States.

Table 2. Allocation of U.S. Security Assistance Funding for the Palestinian Authority Security Sector Reform Programs, Fiscal Years 2007 through 2010 Appropriations (Dollars in millions)

Project area	FY 07 appropriation[a]	FY 08 supplemental appropriation[b]	FY 09 bridge supplemental appropriation[c]	FY 09 appropriation[d]	FY 09 supplemental appropriation[e]	FY 10 appropriation[f]	Total FY 07-10
Training	$28.6	$13.0	$22.6	$13.5	$42.0	$41.0	$160.7
Equipment (non-lethal)	22.6	12.0	0	7.0	30.0	17.0	88.6
Infrastructure	18.6	0	18.4	0	31.0	30.5	98.5
Strategic/capacity development	6.0	0	4.0	3.5	2.0	6.5	22.0
Program development & support[g]	10.6	0	5.0	1.0	1.0	5.0	22.6
Total	$86.4	$25.0	$50.0	$25.0	$106.0	$100.0	$392.4

Source: INL.

Note: All funding shown is from the International Narcotics Control and Law Enforcement appropriations (INCLE) for fiscal years 2007-2010.

[a] Revised Continuing Appropriations Resolution, 2007, Pub. Law No. 110-5, Feb. 5, 2007. Funds from the Economic Support Fund appropriated in Foreign Operations, Export Financing, and Related Programs Appropriations Act, 2006 were transferred and consolidated into the fiscal year 2007 INCLE account pursuant to Presidential Determination No. 2007-11 of January 26, 2007.

[b] Supplemental Appropriations Act, 2008, Pub. Law No. 110-252, June 30, 2008.

[c] Supplemental Appropriations Act, 2008, Pub. Law No. 110-252, June 30, 2008.

[d] Omnibus Appropriations Act, 2009, Pub. Law No. 111-8, March 11, 2009.

[e] Supplemental Appropriations Act, 2009, Pub. Law No. 111-32, June 24, 2009.

[f] Consolidated Appropriations Act, 2010, Pub. Law No. 111-117, Dec. 16, 2009.

[g] Program Development and Support includes overhead items such as salaries, travel, and housing for INL officials, program design costs, and a contribution to the consulate's personal security detail costs, which includes the security escorts and armored vehicles required for travel by U.S. government personnel in the region.

USSC Supports Training Focused Mainly on the NSF

Since 2007, State, primarily through USSC, has allocated more than $160 million to support training of PASF units in Jordan and the West Bank. USSC has focused its training programs mainly on the NSF, and to a lesser extent, the Presidential Guard.

Battalion-Level Training in Jordan

The main component of the USSC training-related activities is battalion-level basic law enforcement and security training conducted at the Jordanian International Police Training Center outside Amman, Jordan. As of January 2010, the Jordanian International Police Training Center had trained four NSF battalions and one Presidential Guard battalion totaling about 2,500 personnel. The trained units include both existing units (Presidential Guard 3rd and NSF 2nd special battalions) and newly recruited battalions (NSF 3rd and 4th special battalions).[20] This training consists of 19 weeks of basic training for all members of a battalion, which usually comprise approximately 500 troops.[21] USSC officials told us that they currently plan to train a total of 10 NSF battalions at the Jordan center. State department officials reported that U.S. security assistance allocated to training from 2007 through 2010 covers the training of 7 of the proposed 10 battalions as shown in figure 3. This would allow one trained NSF special battalion to be deployed in each PA governorate in the West Bank (except in the municipality of Jerusalem, where the PA does not have security control) and one battalion to serve as a reserve for use as needed in any governorate.

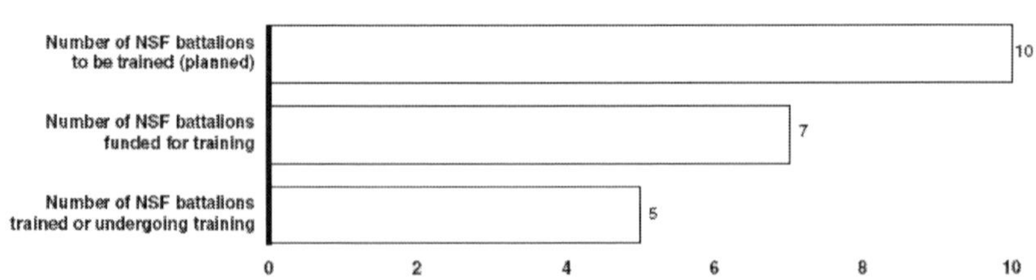

Source: GAO analysis of USSC data.

Figure 3. Status of USSC-Sponsored NSF Battalion Level Training in Jordan as of March 2010.

The basic training includes a mix of classroom and practical exercises focused on the broad areas of firearms operations, crowd control, close quarters operations, patrolling, detainee operations, and checkpoint operations. This training is also designed to help the PA transform and professionalize its security forces by producing well trained, capable graduates able to perform security-related duties supporting the Palestinian Civil Police or other duties as directed by the PA. According to U.S. officials, the training is structured to train by battalion to foster unity of command and build camaraderie among the troops. Although USSC and INL designed the syllabus for this training in consultation with the PA, instructors from Jordan's Public Security Directorate conduct the training under the supervision of INL contractors. According to State and USSC officials, the United States fully vet all troops participating in USSCsponsored training to ensure that no U.S. assistance is provided to or through individuals or entities that advocate, plan, sponsor, engage in, or have engaged in, terrorist activities.[22] In addition, the PA, Israel, and Jordan also vet participants.

Prior to the commencement of each battalion's basic training course, the program trainers conduct three concurrent 4-week preliminary training courses for the battalion's officers, noncommissioned officers, and drivers. These preliminary courses, intended to provide personnel the fundamental skills needed during the battalion training, focus on leadership skills for the officers and noncommissioned officers and advanced driving skills for the drivers. The Jordanian International Police Training Center also offers four 4-week concurrent specialized training courses for select graduates following their completion of the basic training course.

Specialized Training in the West Bank

The USSC also supports and INL funds specialized courses in the West Bank to train and assist members of the NSF special battalions and some other PASF organizations in areas such as leadership, human rights, media awareness, equipment maintenance, and food service operations. Some of the courses continue specialized training for selected members of the NSF battalions that received basic training at the Jordanian International Police Training Center. However, other courses—including a senior leadership course and an intermediate leadership course—are open to all branches of the PA security services. The senior leadership course, first offered in late 2008, is a 2-month course for about 40 commanding officers from all branches of the PASF; as of February 2010, USSC had offered the c ourse 6 times. International trainers taught the initial sessions, and a team comprised of PA and international instructors conducted the most recent senior leadership course. The intermediate leadership course is a new class for middle ranking and noncommissioned officers that adapts principles taught in the senior leaders' course. Altogether, USSC has conducted or supported 24 different specialized courses for PASF personnel in the West Bank between mid-2008 and March 2010, and plans to continue sessions of many of these courses while offering at least two new courses by the end of 20 10. Appendix II provides details on current and planned USSC courses.

Other, smaller U.S. programs train Presidential Guard and Civil Defense troops. In 2008, State's Bureau of Diplomatic Security provided limited training exclusively to the Presidential Guard through its Anti-Terrorism Assistance program.[23] This training focused on police tactical unit operations, leadership development at the middle and senior levels, investigative skills, and crisis response capabilities to enhance the operational effectiveness of the Presidential Guard. Finally, USSC and INL plan to support limited civil defense training for the Palestinian Civil Defense corps at Jordan's regional civil defense training academy.[24]

USSC Provides the NSF and Presidential Guard with Nonlethal Individual and Unit Equipment

Since 2007, State has allocated approximately $89 million to provide nonlethal equipment to 7 NSF battalions and the Presidential Guard. State plans to equip 10 NSF special battalions, as shown in figure 4. USSC is working to ensure that these security forces are properly equipped while garrisoned in their operations camps, and while operating throughout the West Bank. USSC intends to accomplish this by providing an initial issuance of nonlethal equipment to the battalions that have received basic training at the Jordanian International Police Training Center. As of March 2010, the USSC had provided the 3rd Presidential Guard battalion with an initial issuance of equipment, and had provided partial issuances of equipment to the 1st, 2nd, 3rd, and 4th NSF special battalions. State also reported that they have submitted the 5th NSF special battalion's equipment package list to the Israeli government for approval.

USSC and INL, in consultation with the PA, developed the lists of equipment provided to each battalion, which the Government of Israel must also approve. The initial issuance of nonlethal individual and unit equipment for each NSF special battalion includes uniforms with protective gear and operational equipment, including riot shields, batons, and handcuffs as well as computers, tents, basic first aid kits, and support vehicles. (For a list of the specific equipment provided to an NSF battalion see app. III.) USSC also provided the Presidential Guard battalion with a similar initial issuance of nonlethal individual and unit equipment, adapted for their mission specific needs. The USSC and INL also plan to provide search-and-rescue vehicles to the PA civil defense forces.

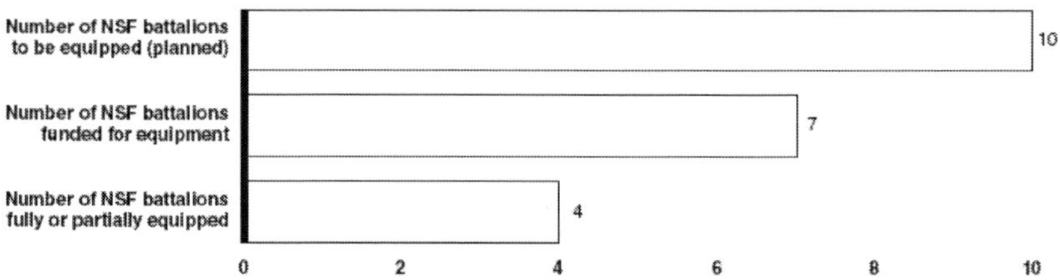

Sources: GAO analysis of INL and USSC data.

Figure 4. Status of USSC-Sponsored NSF Battalion-Level Equipping as of March 2010.

Because all U.S.-provided equipment is subject to end-use monitoring, INL officials and documents note that State maintains the right to examine the property and inspect the records that govern its use. In addition, the United States provided the PA with equipment and training to implement and maintain an inventory system to record and track all U.S. equipment deliveries and disbursements.

USSC Supports Renovation and Construction of PASF Installations

Since 2007, State has allocated approximately $99 million to renovate or construct PASF installations. The main focus of USSC and INL infrastructure activities is to fund and oversee construction of operations camps for 9 of the 10 NSF battalions trained at the Jordanian International Police Training Center.[25] U.S. security assistance allocated to infrastructure from 2007 through 2010 covers the renovation or construction of six of the proposed nine camps (see fig. 5). The operations camps will serve as garrison facilities for the battalion as well as function as a base for conducting operations in the West Bank.

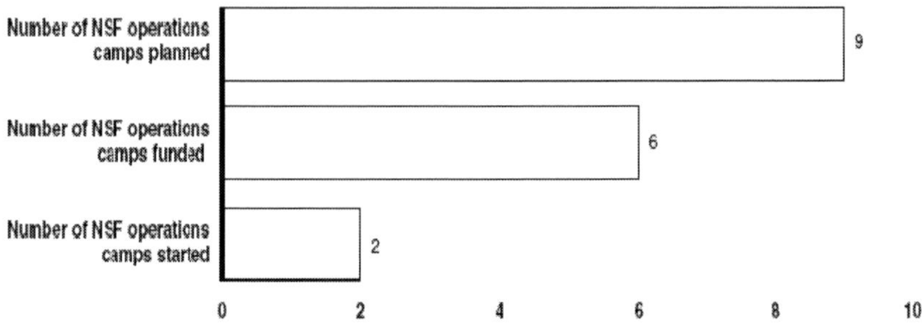

Sources: GAO analysis of INL and USSC data.

Figure 5. Status of USSC- Sponsored NSF Operations Camps as of March 2010.

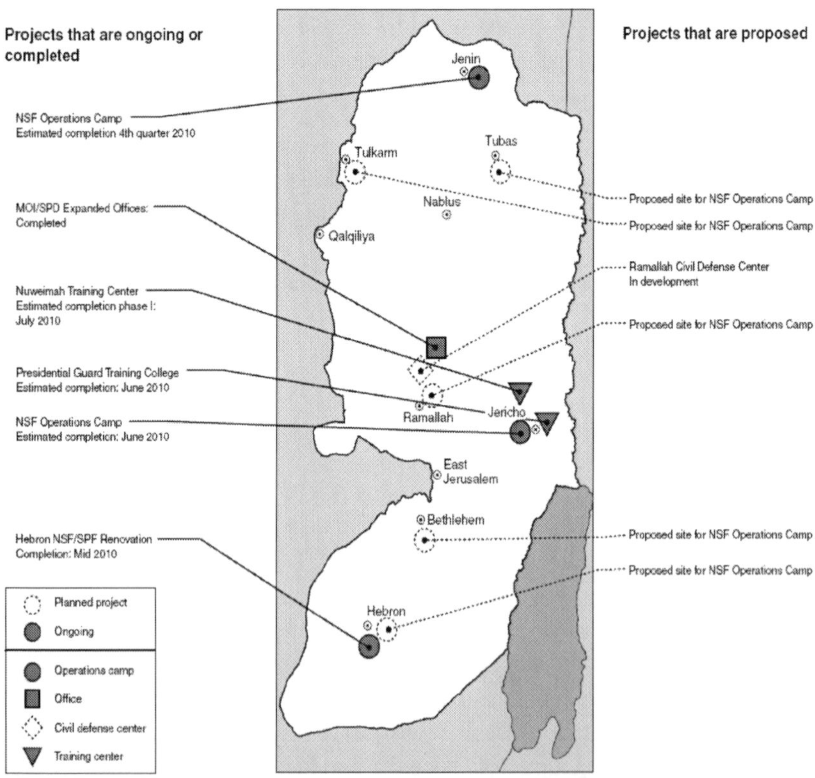

Sources: GAO analysis of USSC data; United Nations (maps).

Figure 6. Map of Planned and Ongoing USSC-funded Infrastructure Projects.

USSC and INL are also funding and overseeing the construction or renovation of training and ministry facilities in the West Bank. Figure 6 shows the six planned and six ongoing or completed infrastructure projects, including the two NSF operations camps, as of March 2010.

The six ongoing or completed infrastructure projects include NSF operations camps, training facilities, and Ministry of Interior facilities, and account for about $41 million of the total allocated for infrastructure. They are in varying stages of completion; however, INL officials expect that all ongoing infrastructure projects will be completed by early 2011.

NSF Operations Camps and Garrison Facilities

- **Jericho NSF Operations Camp**. This operations camp is to serve as the garrison for the 2nd Special Battalion. The camp is to accommodate approximately 750 personnel and provide workspaces, basic vehicle maintenance facilities, parking for approximately 145 squad vehicles and 40 large vehicles, clinical facilities, tactical communications facilities, separate officer berthing and accommodation spaces, a logistic warehouse facility, and K-9 animal housing spaces. State allocated about $11.3 million to this project, which USSC and INL expect to complete by mid-2010. (See figs. 7 and 8.)
- **Jenin NSF Operations Camp**. This operations camp will consist of two barracks buildings that will accommodate approximately 576 troops, one officers' accommodations building that will house over 100 officers, an operational center, mess hall, and gym. State allocated $11 million to this renovation, which USSC and INL officials expect to complete by the end of 2010.
- **Hebron NSF and Special Police Force (SPF) Building**. In this joint NSF and Special Police Force building, the police occupy the ground floor and the NSF the first floor. The goal is to make this building habitable by units from the NSF special battalions deployed to Hebron and make it usable for its intended security functions, including the provision of a safe and secure operating environment, that is capable of being shared with other PA security services. State allocated $170,000 for this renovation, which USSC and INL expect to complete in mid-2010.

Source: GAO photo.

Figure 7. Location of NSF Operations Camp Near Jericho.

Source: GAO photo.

Figure 8. U.S. Funded Construction at the NSF Operations Camp Near Jericho.

Training Facilities

- **Nuweimah Training Center**. The current training facility in Nuweimah is being refurbished and expanded with funding from INL, to serve as an NSF training facility. The facility is to include accommodations for approximately 2,000 troops and 24 classrooms for approximately 1,500 students. The PA's initial plan was to renovate two NSF basic training facilities in Jericho—Nuweimah and Alami. However, according to an INL official the PA and USSC decided not to renovate the Alami site, owing to difficulties in securing needed land titles, and instead to shift all funds to Nuweimah. State allocated about $8 million to this project, which USSC and INL expect to complete by early 2011.
- **Presidential Guard Training College (Jericho)**. The PA intends to use the college to house and train 500 law, order, and security personnel at any given time. This facility has classroom space and accommodations for 250 personnel, as well as dining and support facilities for 500 personnel. State has allocated about $9 million to construct this facility. According to an INL official, original work on the facility was carried out by the UN Office for Project Services, under INL supervision.[26] This facility is currently fully operational, and USSC and INL expect construction to be complete by mid-2010.

Ministry Facilities

- **Ministry of Interior's Strategic Planning Directorate renovation (Ramallah)**. USSC is renovating space in the Ministry of Interior to provide additional office space and a training hub for the Strategic Planning Directorate. The renovation is to add 90 spaces for new staff and two large classrooms, a meeting room, and a security room. State allocated $1.1 million to this renovation, which was completed in February 2010.

To spend the remaining $58 million in infrastructure funding, USSC and INL proposed additional projects, including building NSF operations camps in Hebron, Bethlehem, Ramallah, Tulkarm, Tubas, and a civil defense center in or near Ramallah. However, one U.S. official told us that, because of difficulties in obtaining suitable land and other delays, the USSC is reviewing other options for the NSF operations camps, including constructing temporary operations camps until a permanent site can be identified or renovating existing joint security force facilities to allow them to be used to garrison NSF special battalions. As of March 2010, preliminary design work had begun on a temporary operations camp near Tubas.

USSC Has Centered Capacity Building Programs on Interior Ministry

Since 2007, State has allocated approximately $22 million for capacity-building activities, focused mainly on creating the Ministry of Interior's Strategic Planning Directorate. The Minister of Interior oversees all the security forces reporting to the PA prime minister. According to an INL document, the directorate conducts strategic planning to support security decision making at the executive and ministry level to help the PA establish law and order and facilitate other longer-term security-sector reforms. The directorate is staffed by individuals with strategic planning, logistics capability, and other expertise. According to USSC officials, when Gaza fell to Hamas in mid-2007 and the PA President issued presidential decrees declaring a state of emergency, suspending the current government, and forming a new, more moderate government, the Ministry of Interior lost its entire staff, leaving the newly appointed minister the task of building an entirely new ministry. INL-funded activities include providing technical assistance to the Strategic Planning Directorate, in particular, funding and assigning six international technical advisors to work within the directorate, and training for Ministry and Strategic Planning Directorate staff. According to State documents and officials, as of April 2010, after 2 years of service, the contracts of all six of these advisors had expired, and, at the request of the Minister of Interior, State did not renew them. According to a State official, the Minister of Interior stated in January 2010 that this effort had been concluded to the Ministry's satisfaction, so there are no plans to replace these advisors. He noted that State has offered to make technical assistance available on an ad hoc basis and at the request of the Minister, and, along with other international donors, plans to continue to fund other training and equipping efforts at the Ministry in fiscal year 2011.

In addition to forming the Strategic Planning Directorate, USSC and INL have undertaken other programs to increase the PA's capacity. Examples include the following:

- USSC and INL are providing assistance in building the PA's capacity to coordinate international security assistance. As part of this effort, USSC serves as a technical advisor to a security sector aid-coordinating body co-chaired by the Interior Minister and the government of the United Kingdom.
- USSC and INL are supporting a Canadian-funded effort to develop PASF capacity at the governorate level through the creation of Joint Operations Centers, which are intended to give PASF area commanders in each governorate the command and communications facilities necessary to conduct integrated security operations.
- In support of the PA justice sector, INL launched a $1.5 million small scale justice sector assistance project in Jenin.[27] The program provides technical assistance, training, and modest amounts of equipment to improve capacity of the police to conduct criminal investigations and help the public prosecutor's office manage its caseload. A U.S. official reported that this program could be replicated if successful in other governorates.

Although Improvements in West Bank Security Conditions Have Been Reported, State and USSC Have not Established Clear and Measurable Outcome-Based Performance Indicators

U.S. and international officials have observed improved security conditions in some areas of the West Bank since the PA began deploying units trained and equipped with USSC assistance, although they acknowledge these improvements may not be directly or wholly attributable to USSC programs. However, State and USSC have not assessed how their programs contribute to the achievement of the PA's Roadmap obligations because they have not developed clear and measurable outcome-based performance indicators and targets linking their program activities to stated U.S. program objectives.

Numerous U.S. and International Officials Observed Improved Security Conditions in the West Bank since PA Began Deploying USSC-Trained and Equipped Units

Numerous U.S., PA, Israeli, and other government officials stated that both the PA and the Government of Israel are satisfied with the impact USSC-trained and -equipped PASF battalions have had on improving the security conditions in the West Bank. PA and U.S. officials cited these improvements as examples of how U.S. security assistance is aiding PA progress toward attaining its security obligations under the Roadmap, including having its rebuilt and refocused security apparatus begin sustained, targeted, and effective operations to dismantle terrorist capabilities and infrastructure. These improved conditions include the following.

- **Better PASF capacity to control potentially violent situations**. According to U.S., international, PA and Government of Israel officials, USSC-supported and -trained PASF units contributed successfully to restored security and conducted counterterrorism operations in Jenin, Hebron, Bethlehem, and other areas between 2008 and 2009.[28] Several U.S. and international officials also noted the lack of spontaneous or organized violence in PASF-controlled areas in response to the December 2008 through January 2009 Israeli incursion into Gaza was an indicator of the PASF's growing capacity to anticipate and handle large scale demonstrations and limit potential violence.
- **Fewer Israeli government checkpoints**. Several U.S. officials suggested that the USSC also could point to some indicators as measures of the growing effectiveness of USSC-supported security forces, including the decline in the key manned Israeli security checkpoints in the West Bank. However, the officials stated they could not independently verify the validity or accuracy of the reported declines, nor would they directly attribute these outcomes to USSC activities.[29]
- **Revived economic activity**. According to PA and U.S. officials and documents, the subsequent revival of private investment in Jenin, Hebron, Bethlehem, and other areas where USSC-trained and -equipped PASF battalions were deployed is another indicator that USSC assistance has influenced the security situation, although a

senior PA official noted that PA fiscal policies may have also contributed to this revival.

- **Improved public attitudes toward security forces**. In addition, both State and PA officials noted that Palestinian polling suggests people's views of the PASF have improved, and a State report cited such a poll as indicating growing understanding and confidence of the West Bank populace in their security forces.

State and USSC Officials Have Not Established Clear and Measurable Outcome-based Performance Indicators for PA Security Assistance

Although State and USSC report on PASF program outputs such as the number of personnel vetted, trained, and equipped, USSC has not defined or established outcome-based performance measures to assess the progress, impacts, and estimated costs of achieving USSC objectives. For example, USSC documents and officials note that USSC objectives include helping the PA create right-sized, professional security forces in support of its Roadmap obligations but do not specify measurable outcome-based program performance indicators.[30] USSC and State officials attributed the lack of clear and measurable outcome-based performance indicators and their associated targets for their programs to three factors—(1) changing force requirements, (2) the early stages of PA planning and its limited capacity to rebuild and sustain its security forces, and (3) lack of detailed guidance from State about USSC program objectives, time frames, and reporting requirements.

First, the PA's planned force requirements have undergone several revisions. According to a U.S. official, and as U.S. and PA documents demonstrate, the planned size and composition of the NSF has changed from seven special battalions (five in the West Bank, two in Gaza) in early 2007, to five special battalions solely in the West Bank after the Hamas takeover of Gaza in June 2007. According to State officials and documents, the PA increased the number of battalions for the West Bank from five to seven by mid-2008, although the projected total number of personnel remained at 3,500 as each battalion was reduced in size from 700 to 500 personnel in part to create smaller units better suited for the urban environment in which they would operate. In 2009, the PA raised the projected size of the NSF to 10 special battalions, according to USSC officials.[31] Some State officials and documents also noted that the PASF has not clarified the role of the

Presidential Guard and that some of its units had assumed gendarmerie tasks beyond its original mandate, which may overlap with NSF responsibilities.

The revised and unclear requirements reflect that the parties to the Roadmap agreement—the PA and Israel—have not agreed on common measures to assess progress in meeting their Roadmap security obligations, according to USSC officials. For example, a September 2008 USSC report noted that the Government of Israel and the PA have not developed "effects-based metrics" needed to define a successful PASF security or counterterrorism effort under the Roadmap.[32] State officials stated that the Government of Israel prefers not to establish objectives or measures that might limit its flexibility to conduct security operations within the West Bank.

Second, the PA's plans and capacity to reform, rebuild, and sustain its security forces are still in a relatively early stage of development.[33] As a result, State and USSC officials said it is difficult to set outcome-based targets to measure the progress or outcomes of their programs. For example, the PA's capacity to direct its own transformation was lacking until recently. According to a senior PA official, the Minister of the Interior did not consolidate within the ministry the authority to request, accept, and coordinate all foreign donor security assistance until August 2009.

Third, USSC officials said that State did not give USSC a "blueprint" for attaining defined and measurable objectives for its programs within a set period of time, or for estimating the amount and type of resources needed to achieve such USSC goals as aiding in the transformation of the PA security sector and the creation of a professional, right-sized security force. According to State, this stemmed from the absence of a requirements-based budget allocation process for USSC programs until 2008. Since then, however, State officials said they required USSC and INL to provide performance indicators beginning with the fiscal year 2009 Jerusalem mission strategic plan. Furthermore, a senior USSC official said they had little incentive to emphasize or develop performance targets because State had shown little interest in tracking performance in the past; in fact, regular monthly reports from USSC to State on its activities resumed only in November 2009 after a hiatus of more than a year.

Despite these factors, deriving indicators to measure and manage performance against an agency's results-oriented goals has been identified by GAO as good management practice because it would help provide objective and useful performance information for decision makers when faced with limited resources and competing priorities.[34] GAO has previously reported that while agency managers encounter difficulties in setting outcome-oriented goals or collecting useful data on expected results in general, it is difficult to design effective strategies or measure the impact of programs without them.[35] State and USSC officials noted that USSC was developing a campaign plan for release in mid-2010 to help the Palestinians implement their own revised security strategy—which was still not released as of March 2010–and expected the plan to incorporate performance indicators to the extent possible. According to U.S. military doctrine, effective planning cannot occur without a clear understanding of the desired end state and the conditions that must exist to in order to end the operation. Moreover, a campaign plan should provide an estimate of the time and forces required to reach the conditions for mission success or termination. Determining when conditions are met requires "measures of effectiveness," such as outcome-based performance measures.[36] GAO has reported on the importance of outcome-based performance indicators as a key characteristic of effective national security strategy planning and a necessary component of developing and executing campaign plans based on these strategies (see list of related GAO products at end of report).

Although the fiscal year 2010 Jerusalem mission strategic plan identifies performance indicators for U.S. security assistance programs, the targets to measure progress towards achieving these indicators focus on program outputs rather than program outcomes. For example, the plan identified the performance indicator "building Palestinian security capabilities" to assess progress toward achieving State's broader goal of reforming Palestinian security forces to improve law and order and reduce terrorism.[37] However, this indicator is measured based on output targets such as "completing the training and equipping of at least one PG and one NSF battalion" in fiscal year 2008 rather than on outcomes such as reduced terrorism as measured by, for example, changes in the number of terrorist-related incidents or changes in crime rates. Moreover, neither the performance plan nor USSC documents establish measurable outcome targets for assessing progress towards such stated USSC objectives as creating a "right-sized, professional" security force or helping the PA transform its security sector. Nor do these plans and documents contain information on expected time frames or estimated total costs for achieving these goals.[38]

State and USSC officials acknowledged that it would be useful to describe the impacts of U.S. security assistance on such outcomes as reductions in the number of Israeli security checkpoints in the West Bank. Similarly, they acknowledged it would be useful to tailor some survey questions to establish baselines and assess over time the extent to which polling data suggesting growing Palestinian confidence in their security can be attributed to the conduct and actions of USSC-trained PASF personnel, but noted the difficulty in separating the impact of U.S. security assistance from the impact of such external factors as Israeli political and security actions. In March 2010, State and USSC officials said that they had tasked an officer to clarify how USSC activities achieve State objectives and to improve reporting on USSC performance.

U.S. Security Assistance Programs Face Logistical Constraints and Outpace Development of the Rule of Law

Logistical constraints on personnel movement and access, equipment delivery, and acquisition of land for infrastructure projects challenge the implementation of U.S. security assistance programs. In addition, State, USSC, and international officials and documents note that programs to develop the capacity of the civil police and the justice sector are not proceeding at the same pace as U.S. security sector reform programs.

U.S. Security Assistance Faces Several Logistical Constraints

Logistical constraints—largely outside U.S. control–involving personnel movement and access, equipment approval and delivery, and land acquisition challenge the implementation of U.S. security assistance in the West Bank and Gaza.

Constraints on Personnel Movement and Access

State travel restrictions and Israeli Defense Force security checkpoints limit the movement and access of U.S. personnel into and within the West Bank. State restricts U.S. government personnel travel into and within the West Bank and requires that they travel in armored vehicles with security teams when traveling to State designated high threat areas. However, such restrictions do not apply to personnel from other countries supporting the USSC, such as the United Kingdom and Canada, according to State officials. As a result, according to U.S. officials, USSC relies on non-U.S. personnel to visit Palestinian security leaders on a daily basis, gauge local conditions, and conduct training in the West Bank. Israeli security checkpoints when traveling into and out of the West Bank border also limit U.S. government personnel movement and access, according to U.S. officials. For example, on more than one occasion, U.S. government delegations, including staff from USSC and State, were prevented from entering or exiting the West Bank, according to USSC and State officials. PA officials also face movement and access difficulties crossing at Israeli checkpoints when traveling into and out of the West Bank, which hampers the ability of USSC to meet with PA outside of the West Bank.

Delays in Equipment Approval and Delivery

While a process exists for equipment approval and delivery as shown in figure 9, U.S. officials said problems affecting the approval and delivery of equipment have hampered USSC's ability to equip the PASF in a timely manner. USSC officials noted that without a significant effort at a higher political level to streamline this process, delays will frequently occur with little recourse available to USSC.

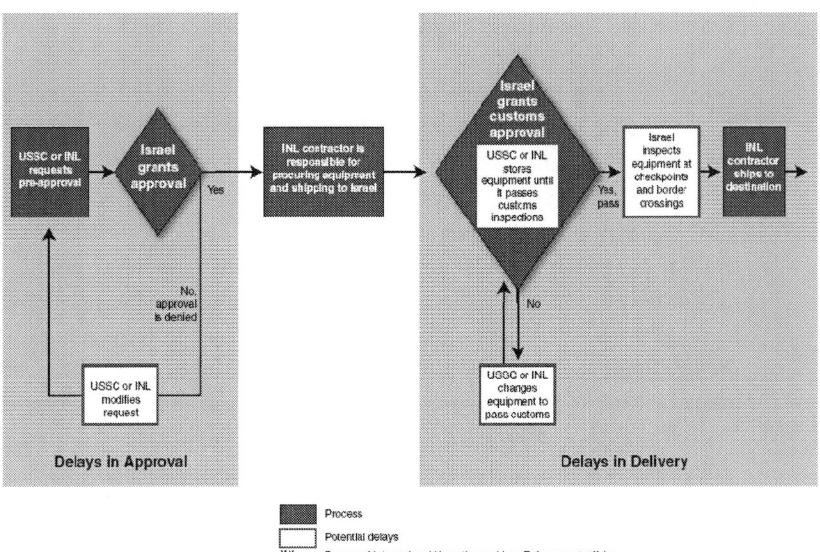

Source: GAO analysis of USSC data.

Figure 9. Process for Equipment Approval and Delivery.

Delays in equipment approval and delivery have occurred throughout this process, for example:

- **Delays in approval.** An absence of agreed-upon terms for the approval of equipment requests, such as equipment specifications or a set timeframe to make approval decisions, has resulted in delayed Israeli approval of shipments of USSC and other donor equipment, according to U.S. and other donor officials.[39] For example, State and EU donor officials told us that the Government of Israel has not agreed to specific procedures for pre-approval of equipment orders as it prefers to continue to approve or deny each equipment request on a case-by-case basis. According to an Israeli official, each equipment request must be reviewed on its own merits, as specifications can change. For example, an Israeli official stated that although the Government of Israel had approved procurement of a shipment of raincoats, it did not guarantee the approval of future shipments of raincoats of comparable types and quantities. In addition, because the parties have not agreed on time frames for submitting or approving equipment requests, significant differences between the amounts of time needed to approve various items have constrained USSC's ability to estimate equipment delivery dates. For instance, some vehicles ordered for the Presidential Guard and NSF 2nd Special Battalion in March 2008 were delivered in June 2008 while others were not delivered until January 2009. On the other hand, USSC officials said in March 2010 that the time needed to complete the approval process has declined from approximately 3 months to 2 weeks for items that had been approved in prior shipments by the Israeli government. Nevertheless, these officials note there is no guarantee that previously approved items will continue to be approved by the Government of Israel. For example, they noted that as of November 2009 INL has paid at least $176,000 to store a $2.3 million shipment of approximately 1,400 radios and associated gear that the Israeli government approved for delivery, but was then impounded by Israeli customs upon arrival in port in early 2009 after the Government of Israel revoked this approval.[40]
- **Delays in delivery.** Delays have occurred at Israeli customs and during shipment into the West Bank, constraining USSC's mission of properly equipping the NSF and Presidential Guard, according to officials we spoke with. USSC officials stated that shipping items to

Israel takes about 1 month by sea and as little as 1 day by air from the United States. However, USSC officials also stated that while the time needed for Israeli customs to approve shipments averages about 2 months, approval can take up to a year or more for items that require modification by the Israelis in order to pass Israeli customs inspections. For example, USSC officials noted that vehicles and trailers were held up as Israeli customs required modifications to their lights, brakes, and other specifications before they would release them. According to an Israeli official, the PA also contributes to the equipment delays at customs by not following the shipment instructions in the approved requests. For example, in one case equipment was shipped with other types of goods destined for the West Bank and the quantity of equipment was lower than the approved amount. In another case, the shipper consolidated a shipment of PASF items with items for other customers. The increasing number of equipment deliveries in 2009 has also added to the delays in clearing customs, according to the Israeli government official. Additional unexpected delays in delivery have occurred when Israeli customs inspectors have not released equipment shipments they have approved, according to USSC and INL officials.[41] These officials told us that security inspections required at Israeli border crossings and checkpoints in the West Bank have also delayed delivery. USSC and INL officials noted that they have taken steps to improve their ability to deliver equipment on time, including: developing standardized NSF battalion equipment packages to minimize Israeli opportunities to question equipment specifications; requiring the contracted freight forwarder in Virginia to check every item against shipment manifests prior to shipment; and making greater use of airfreight delivery. In addition, USSC officials said they have shortened the lead times needed to procure and ship equipment over time by pre-ordering items previously approved by the Israelis to be included in later shipments.

Moreover, USSC, INL, and PA officials and staff have found it difficult to check on the status of the shipment or to hold parties accountable for delays, according to USSC officials. These officials stated that conflict appears to exist between various Israeli government departments related to the equipping process, which periodically results in unexplained delays in equipment release or approval. According to USSC, it is unclear with whom USSC or PA officials should speak to seek redress for unexplained equipment delays; as a result, delays are often elevated to high level U.S. and Israeli officials, who then negotiate a resolution. These delays have hampered USSC's ability to equip the trained NSF and Presidential Guard battalions in a timely manner. While the USSC planned to deliver equipment to these battalions upon their graduation from JIPTC, some of these battalions have operated for several months after graduation without all of their needed equipment. For example, INL ordered equipment for the PG 3rd battalion and NSF 2nd special battalion in December 2007 to be distributed at the time of their May 2008 graduation; however, USSC and INL officials noted that although these two battalions had received all of their vehicles as of March 2010, they had yet to receive 14 percent of their equipment. As of March 2010, the 3rd and 4th NSF special battalions that had completed training in Jordan prior to December 2010 had received over 90 percent of their vehicles but only 44 to 50 percent of their other equipment, according to State officials. These officials said that the 1st NSF special battalion, which graduated in January 2010, had not received any of the purchased vehicles and only 2 percent of its other equipment as of March 2010.[42]

INL officials stated that these equipment shortfalls had not significantly affected the ability of the NSF special battalions to operate once they were deployed back to the West Bank. However, they acknowledged that these units had been deployed to the field lacking critical items, such as helmets, armored vests, and communications gear, that had been proposed, and in some cases procured, by the USSC and INL but had not been approved for delivery by the government of Israel.

Constraints on Land Acquisition

The completion of U.S.-funded infrastructure projects has been delayed by constraints on acquiring land in the West Bank that are largely outside of U.S. control, according to USSC, INL, and PA officials. Israel must approve the location of all proposed facilities and does not set formal standards by which locations are approved, according to USSC officials. These officials also said the PA is largely limited to building in Oslo Area A, which is solely under PA authority but comprises less than 20 percent of the West Bank's territory. USSC officials also stated that it is difficult to determine whether a proposed installation site includes land solely in Area A. In addition, the Government of Israel requires that the proposed installation sites must not be near Israeli settlements or access routes. After the Government of Israel approves an installation site, USSC officials stated they face a lengthy Palestinian process for establishing ownership rights and obtaining legal title to the land. These officials noted that conflicting land and property claims on the site also create a challenge to acquiring land for PA infrastructure projects. Figure 10 depicts areas where the PA usually can acquire land for security installations in the West Bank (area A) and areas where it cannot (areas B and C).

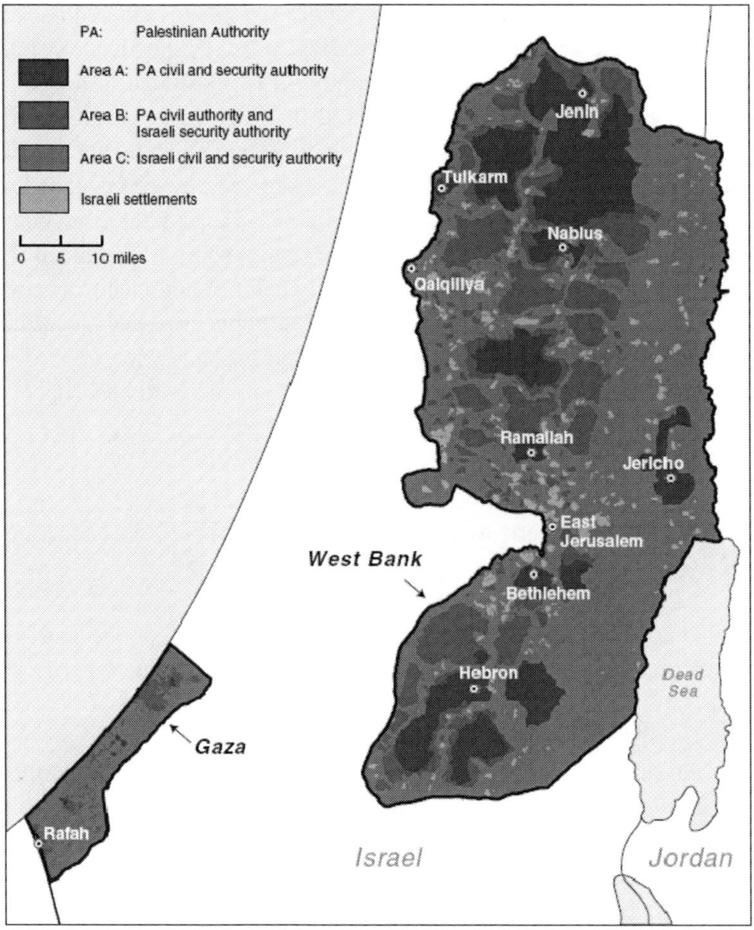

Sources: GAO analysis of USSC data; United Nations (maps).

Figure 10. Division of West Bank Territory by Oslo Area of Control and Israeli Settlements (2009).

Because of these restrictions and delays, USSC and INL officials said efforts to develop NSF operations camps beyond the two already under construction remain stalled as of March 2010. Owing to delays in acquiring suitable land for permanent camps and the need to house newly trained battalions, USSC and INL officials said they have built temporary operations camps. Similarly, because of delays in land acquisition, USSC and INL cancelled renovation plans of an NSF facility in Alami and redirected the funding to the Nuweimah facility, according to an INL official. Originally designed to house 700 trainees, Nuweimah will be expanded to house 2,000 trainees upon completion in fiscal year 2011. To work around restricted property in certain urban areas, the USSC and INL are planning to construct or renovate multistory buildings within urban-based security compounds known as muquata'as. This effort is underway or being planned for compounds in Tulkarm and other urban locations. As a result, some U.S.-funded PASF centers are holding more troops than originally planned and facilities are being built in a way that allows them to be expanded upon if needed, according to USSC and INL officials. These land acquisition problems constrain USSC's goal to provide housing for each of the NSF special battalions upon their completion of training in Jordan.

Capacity Development of PA Civil Police and Justice Sector Is Limited

U.S. and international officials noted that PA civil police and justice sector reforms are not proceeding at the same pace as U.S. security sector reforms.

- Palestinian Civil Police (PCP) capacity is limited. According to EUPOL COPPS advisors, the PCP lags behind all other Palestinian security forces in funding for infrastructure and equipment. Although infrastructure exists, such as joint operation centers and prison facilities, about 60 new police stations need to be rebuilt or constructed and existing facilities need to be refurbished, according to a USSC document. The PCP also have difficulties obtaining certain types of equipment, such as finger printing equipment, radios, and personal protective equipment, according to EUPOL COPPS. Also, the judicial police—charged with serving court orders, protecting judges and judicial facilities, and transporting prisoners—lack vehicles and operating capabilities outside of Ramallah, according to a USSC report. According to a U.S. official, a decision was made in 2008 to increase the size of the NSF in the West Bank from 5 to 10 NSF special battalions in part to compensate for the lack of PCP capacity.

- According to State and international officials, the NSF and the PCP do not coordinate programs to a large extent. Although the NSF receives training on operating with the PCP at JIPTC and PCP are trained on operating with NSF at many different levels, including at USSC-sponsored courses, the NSF and PCP coordination needs to be strengthened, according to U.S. and other officials. While an INL official said the PA is taking efforts to increase coordination between these two security forces through the Interior Ministry's Strategic Planning Directorate, the PCP's lack of communication equipment, such as radios, limits coordination. A EUPOL COPPS official told us that it is difficult for the PCP to obtain radios and frequencies and such a lack of communication equipment constrains the building of a sophisticated and well-equipped civil police force.
- Justice sector capacity is limited. The PA justice sector still lacks sufficient infrastructure, organization, and updated laws, according to PA, U.S., and international documents and officials.[43] Justice-sector infrastructure, such as facilities and courts in each governorate, require upgrades and improvements by 2011, according to USSC. U.S. and foreign officials told us that to improve justice-sector organization, the PA needs to more clearly define the roles of its government agencies. According to a USSC report, cooperation between the elements of the criminal justice system—the courts, police, and prosecutors—is poor. In addition, USSC reported that the physical separation of government agencies within and between governorates results in poor coordination.[44] USSC further reported that the lack of clarity and consistency in PA laws and the lack of a working legislature also undermine PA civil police and justice-sector capacity. USSC reported that the PASF, including the civil police, are constrained in their ability to conduct security operations and to detain persons who present a security threat and the justice sector is constrained in convicting such persons because Palestinian laws on some related issues are vague and sometimes contradictory. However, such laws cannot be reviewed and updated until after a new Palestinian Legislative Council is installed.[45]

- Moreover, a State document noted that the civil police and justice-sector capacity limitations have become a matter of greater concern as it has become apparent that other donors are not providing the necessary civil policing, justice-sector, and other pledged assistance necessary to keep pace with the progress the U.S. security assistance programs are achieving. According to U.S. and PA officials and documents, sustaining the progress they have made with U.S. assistance in the security sector may be difficult unless the lack of capacity in the civil police and the justice sectors with which the USSC-supported security forces must operate are addressed. To help address some of these gaps, State officials said State had recently reinforced its role for facilitating coordination among U.S. agencies and international donors for justice-sector issues. Examples of U.S. and international justice-sector reform programs include: the INL's Justice Sector Assistance Project, USAID's Rule of Law and Justice Enforcement Program, EUPOL COPPS' civil police and rule of law program, and the Canadian International Development Agency's "Sharaka" Program, as shown in table 3.

Table 3. Select PA Justice-Sector Reform Programs

Donor/program	Description
U.S. INL Justice Sector Assistance Project	Improve the capacity of the Jenin justice sector, primarily the police and public prosecution, to investigate and prosecute cases to reduce the current case backlog through technical assistance, training, and modest amounts of equipment. Plans to expand program to strengthen cooperation between criminal investigators and prosecutors.
USAID Rule of Law and Justice Enforcement Program	Build the management capacity and case management system of the courts and increase publicconfidence in the justice sector through outreach programs.
EUPOL COPPS	Advise and monitor the functioning of the PA justice sector through the Civil Police, the Ministry of Justice, the prosecutor's offices, and courts.
Canadian International Development Agency "Sharaka" Program	Provide training, equipment, infrastructure, information technology systems, and support to the Office of Attorney General and the Public Prosecution Service. Also provide support to forensics and courthouses.

Source: GAO analysis of U.S. and international program documents.

Conclusion

In fiscal years 2007 through 2010, State allocated approximately $392 million in USSC assistance to support U.S. strategic goals and Roadmap objectives in the Middle East, and has requested $150 million more for fiscal year 2011. Most of this assistance has supported training and equipping new PASF battalions deployed in the West Bank. Although U.S. and international officials said that U.S. security assistance has helped the PA improve security conditions in some areas of the West Bank and is progressing faster than PA civil police and justice sector reforms, State and USSC have not established clear and measurable outcome-based performance indicators to assess and report on the progress of their security assistance. As such, it is difficult for State and the USSC to gauge whether or not their security assistance programs are helping the PA achieve its Roadmap obligations to undertake security sector transformation and create a right-sized, professional security force. Establishing and tracking outcome-based performance measures in the proposed USSC campaign plan would help inform decisions about the costs, progress, and impact of U.S. security assistance to the PA particularly given that this assistance is progressing faster than the PA civil police and justice-sector reforms.

Recommendations

As State develops the USSC campaign plan for providing security assistance to the PA, we recommend that the Secretary of State establish outcome-based indicators and track them over time. State should define specific program objectives and identify appropriate outcome-based indicators that would demonstrate progress toward achieving those objectives, and would enable it to, among other things, weigh the progress made in developing the security forces, civil police, Ministry of Interior, and justice sectors.

Agency Comments

State provided written comments on a draft of this report, which are reprinted in appendix IV. State partially concurred with our recommendation that the Secretary of State establish outcome-based indicators and track them over time. State commented that they recognize the need for such indicators and have tried to develop ones that are meaningful at this stage of the program's development. For example, State mentioned that they have included broad performance measures in the Mission Strategic Plan. INL has also factored performance measures into all of its funding obligating documents. State, however, accepts our point that these measures should be more performance-based. Now that trained and equipped security force units are in place, State anticipates developing meaningful security-related baseline data for measuring the progress of U.S. sponsored trained units. State further commented that they have already started to do this with the Jenin justice project, whereby the PA will be able to generate comparative data on the number, speed, and success of the cases they prosecute. In addition, State commented that INL is in the process of crafting a new Letter of Agreement with the Palestinian Authority. This letter is to contain project goals, objectives, and milestones that reflect the program's recent and anticipated future growth in size and complexity.

State cautioned that, as we reported, several factors outside of State's control influence progress toward the most meaningful performance-based indicators. State noted that while security assistance provided by the United States can strengthen the capabilities of the Palestinian security forces to operate increasingly in certain areas, the Palestinian Authority will only be able to do so if it and the Government of Israel agree on the direction and pace of this deployment. Ultimately, State added, such an agreement depends on a range of political, economic, and social factors that encompass more than just the enhanced law enforcement and security capabilities U.S. assistance gives the PA security forces. State also provided technical comments that we incorporated, as appropriate.

We are sending copies of this report to interested congressional committees and the Secretary of State. In addition, the report will be available at no charge on the GAO Web site at http://www.gao.gov.

If you or any of your staffs have any question about this report, please contact me at (202) 512-3149 or gootnickd@gao.gov. Contact points for our Offices of Congressional Relations and Public Affairs may be found on the last page of this report. GAO staff who made major contribution to this report are listed in appendix V.

David Gootnick
Director, International Affairs and Trade.

Appendix I: Scope and Methodology

To describe the nature and extent of U.S. security assistance to the Palestinian Authority since 2007, we reviewed relevant documents and interviewed officials from the Departments of State (State) and Defense (DOD), the Office of the United States Security Coordinator (USSC), and the U.S. Agency for International Development (USAID) in Washington, D.C., in the West Bank, at the U.S. Consulate in Jerusalem, and the U.S. Embassies in Tel Aviv and Amman, Jordan. We also met with PA, Israeli, and Jordanian government and security officials as well as recognized experts in Israeli-Palestinian affairs. We reviewed State's Bureau of International Narcotics and Law Enforcement Affairs (INL) budget justifications for fiscal years 2008 through 2010 to determine the levels of International Narcotics and Law Enforcement (INCLE) funding allocated to USSC and INL security assistance programs in the West Bank. We determined that the INCLE funding allocation data was sufficiently reliable for our purposes.

To describe the nature and extent of the training programs, we reviewed INL, USSC, and contractor status report documentation and conducted site visits to observe U.S.-sponsored training at the Jordanian International Police Training Center. We reviewed examples of training reports, student surveys, and after action reports used by USSC contractors to review the performance of their trainees during and after every National Security Forces (NSF) training session. To describe the status of USSC programs to equip the NSF, we reviewed equipment delivery lists, contractor statements of work, equipment delivery work orders, and summaries of equipment end use monitoring reports. We interviewed INL, USSC, Palestinian Authority Security Forces (PASF), and Jordanian officials about the status of equipment deliveries. To describe the status of the construction of PASF installations, we reviewed the August 2007 "Framework Agreement" signed between the Secretary of State and the PA Prime Minister as well as INL contract summary data and progress reports; visited construction projects in and around the city of Jericho; and interviewed PA and INL contract staff about project objectives, plans, and funding issues. We assessed the reliability of the data on the battalions trained and equipped by the USSC, and on the infrastructure construction data provided by INL. We did not assess the reliability of the data on the current size and structure of the PASF because we are presenting them for background purposes only.

To assess State's efforts to measure the effectiveness of its security assistance programs, we examined whether its approach identified and applied measurable performance indicators necessary to gauge results—as called for in a number of GAO products listed at the end of this report. These reports state that developing and applying outcome-based performance indicators are (1) a management best practice; (2) one of the key characteristics of effective national security strategy planning, particularly when developing counterterrorism strategies; and (3) a necessary component of developing and executing campaign plans based on these strategies. We also reviewed other GAO reports assessing the extent to which other U.S. assistance projects develop and apply results-based performance indicators. We reviewed the strategic plans for State's Bureau of Near Eastern Affairs and the mission performance and the mission strategic plans for the U.S. Consulate in Jerusalem for fiscal years 2009 through 2011, as well as the four monthly activity reports the USSC has produced between November 2009 and March 2010. We examined United Nations Office for Coordination of Humanitarian Affairs data and an Israeli Ministry of Defense report for changes in the number of Israeli roadblocks within the West Bank from 2007 to 2009.

To determine factors that may affect the implementation of U.S. security assistance to the Palestinian Authority, we analyzed reports, conference presentations, and U.S. government sponsored studies to identify issues that affect U.S. programs. We conducted interviews with State, INL, and USSC officials in Washington, D.C., and in the field. We also met with Israeli, PA, Jordanian, and other international officials during our fieldwork in Israel, the West Bank, Jerusalem, and Jordan. To assess logistical constraints, we reviewed relevant UN and State documents on access and movement; INL and USSC documents on the logistics of providing equipment to the PA; and met with USSC officials to discuss challenges in acquiring land for U.S.- funded infrastructure in the West Bank. To illustrate the U.S.-funded equipment approval and delivery process, we developed a schematic representation and identified points during which the process may experience problems based on discussions with U.S., Israeli, and PA officials. We consulted with INL and USSC officials and incorporated their comments into our representation of the equipment approval and delivery process. To assess the capacity of the PA police and justice sector and its impact on U.S. security assistance, we reviewed documents from and met with USSC, Israeli, PA, and international officials. To examine the pace of U.S. and international assistance to the PA civil police and justice sector, we also reviewed State documents and met with current PA police and justice sector donors, including USAID, INL, and EUPOL COPPS.

We conducted our work from July 2009 to May 2010 and in accordance with generally accepted government auditing standards. Those standards require that we plan and perform the audit to obtain sufficient, appropriate evidence to provide a reasonable basis for our findings and conclusions based on our audit objectives. We believe that the evidence obtained provides a reasonable basis for our findings and conclusions based on our audit objectives.

APPENDIX II: LIST OF USSC COURSES PROVIDED TO THE PASF IN THE WEST BANK, JULY 2008 TO MARCH 2010

Table 4 shows the 24 different specialized courses the USSC has conducted or supported for PASF personnel in the West Bank between mid-2008 and March 2010, and the two additional courses it planned to offer as of March 2010.

Table 4. USSC-Sponsored Training Courses in the West Bank, July 2008 – March 2010

Course title	Approximate course length	Start date	Approximate number trained
PASF Senior Leaders Course	60 days	Oct. 2008	6 courses held with selected PASF personnel
PASF Intermediate Leaders Course	30 days	Feb. 2010	2 courses held with selected PASF personnel
Human Rights/Use of Force	35 hours	Mar. 2010	40 PASF students
HQ Staff Training	30 days	July 2008	Selected staff from 4 NSF battalions
Advanced Staff Training	30 days	Oct. 2008	Selected staff from 3 NSF battalions
Intermediate English Language Training	10 weeks	Sept. 2008	86 students
Advanced English Language Training	10 weeks (or 5 weeks intensive)	Nov. 2008	108 students
Map Reading and Symbols	30 days	July 2009	40 NSF students
Media Awareness Training	30 days	March 2010	20 PASF students
Medical Refresher Training	30 days	Feb. 2009	Selected personnel from 4 NSF battalions

Table 4. (Continued)

Course title	Approximate course length	Start date	Approximate number trained
Basic Lifesaver First Aid	5 days	Nov. 2009	80 students
First Responder	6-8 weeks	Dec. 2009	80 students
Tactical Logistics	30 days	June 2009	Selected personnel from 3 NSF battalions
Basic Driver Training	30 days	Oct. 2008	Selected personnel from 3 NSF battalions, 120 NSF students, 120 PASF students
Vehicle Maintenance	30 days	March 2009	Selected personnel from 3 battalions
15 Ton Drivers Training	15 weeks	Nov. 2009	30 NSF students
Recovery Vehicle Training	3-4 months	May 2009	Selected personnel from 3 NSF battalions
Fleet Management	30 days	Dec. 2008	Selected personnel from 3 NSF battalions
Equipment Maintenance	30 days	Nov. 2009	Selected personnel from 1 NSF battalion
Warehouse Management	30 days	Feb. 2009	Selected personnel from 4 NSF battalions
Training/Training Management	N/A	Planned	N/A
Communications Training	30 days	March 2010	150 NSF students
Communications Maintenance	4 months	March 2010	None complete as of March 31, 2010
Computer Skills Training	30 days	Dec. 2009	20 students
Food Service Operations	4 months	Feb. 2010	None complete as of March 31, 2010
Nutrition Training	3 months	Planned	None complete as of March 31, 2010

Source: GAO analysis of USSC data.

APPENDIX III: USSC LIST OF EQUIPMENT APPROVED FOR PROVISION TO THE NSF 3RD AND 4TH BATTALIONS

Table 5 shows the type and quantity of equipment approved for the NSF 3rd and 4th battalions. USSC procures an initial issuance of equipment for battalions trained with U.S. funds at the Jordanian International Police

Training Center adjusting the issuance slightly for each battalion. An average battalion consists of 500 troops.

Table 5. Equipment Approved for Provision to the NSF 3rd and 4th Battalions

Description	Quantity
Vehicles	
Ambulances	3
4-Door Sedan (Surveillance vehicle)	8
Isuzu D-MAX 4x4 Supercrew Truck	64
Benches, rack systems and tarps for Isuzu D-MAX	64
3500 Truck, Diesel 4x4	15
3500 Truck, Diesel 4x4	15
Prisoner transport van (Paddy Wagon)	2
Tow Truck	2
Generator trailer	4
Water trailer, 500 gallon	5
Tool Box, truck mounted	2
Organizational (Recon Platoon)	
Video camera/Camcorder (No tape)	4
4GB Memory stick for cameras, camcorders	8
Camera	4
10 X 50 Binoculars	16
Speciality Equipment	
Extendable mirror	12
Rappelling gloves	68
Grenadier gloves	15
Rappelling harness system	68
Police Entry Equipment	
Dual Handled Entry Sledge/Door Ram	6
Climbing Rope	10
Climbing Ladders	10
Brean-N-Rake Entry Bar for windows	6
Dynamic Entry Back Kit (cutters, sledge, bar)	6
Close Quarter Dynamic Entry Sledge	6
Hydraulic Spreaderbar (doorway)	6
Gorilla Entry Bar (doorway)	6
Ballistic Entry Shield (Level IIIA)	6
Fence Climbing Kit	6
Dynamic Entry Sledge (Regular)	6
Ladder, Telescopic	6
General Equipment	

Table 5. (Continued)

Description	Quantity
Mobile Light Trailer	10
Handheld Spot Lights (rechargable)	100
Road Cones	100
Metal Bars for checkpoints	50
Spike Strips	30
Metal Detectors	24
Steel Handcuffs	500
Head Flashlights (rechargable)	550
Bullhorns	10
Camera, Snake	6
Handheld Monitor	6
Spotting Scope with camera adapter	4
Rubber training mat	1
Printer	5
Scanner/Fax	4
Copier Machine	2
Projectors	4
Wallboards	14
Paper Shredder	3
DVD Player/VCR	6
Laminator	2
Laptops	6
Desktops	6
Water Coolers	30
Television	6
Road Emergency Kit (triangle, fire ext., reflective vest)	64
Rain Tarp	15
Washer and Dryer	1
Medical Equipment	
Tactical Trauma Kit	15
First Responder Kit	120
Resuscitation Mannequin	2
Litter, Non-Rigid Poleless	20
Litter, Folding Rigid Aluminum Nylon	8
Litter, Stand	8
Litter, Straps	6
First Aid Kits, small, individual, with case	550
Riot Gear	
Riot Shield	300
Riot Helmet	300

Description	Quantity
Riot Gloves	300
Knee Pads	300
Elbow Pads	300
Riot Control Gas Mask	300
Gas Mask Cartridges (2 per person)	600
Riot Baton	300
Individual Equipment	
Helmets, Level I	550
Body Armor, Level II	550
Uniforms	
PT Gear (shorts, shirt, track suit, shoes, socks)	550
Field Jacket	550
Rain Suit	550
Patch, Palestinian flag	1,100
Patch, NSF	1,100
Patch, Battalion	1,100
Patch, eagle logo, on beret	550
Boots	1,100
Beret	550
Ball cap, BDU	550
Military sweater	550
Coveralls	20
Cold Weather Suit	550
Undershirt, Cotton, Green (3 per person)	1,650
Undershirt, CW Green, POLYPRO	550
Trousers, Green, 70% cotton (2 per person)	1,100
Shirt, Green with pockets, 70% cotton (2 per person)	1,100
Socks, black, 100% cotton (3 pairs per person)	1,650
Scarf, wool, knit	550
Drawers, Olive drab, 100% cotton (3 per person)	1,650
Drawers, CW POLYPRO	550
Cap, watch, black, fleece	550
Standard Issue	
Sleeping bag	550
Tactical Vest	550
Canteens, with case	550
Mission bag	550
Tent, GP Medium	20
Web belts	1,050
Foam sleeping pad	550
Poncho liner	550
Bag, Duffle	550

Table 5. (Continued)

Description	Quantity
Bag, barracks (laundry)	550
Cup, canteen	550
Towels	1,050
Bag, waterproof	550
Sheets	1,000

Source: USSC.

APPENDIX IV: STATE COMMENTS ON DRAFT REPORT

United States Department of State

Chief Financial Officer

Washington, D.C. 20520

APR 26 2010

Ms. Jacquelyn Williams-Bridgers
Managing Director
International Affairs and Trade
Government Accountability Office
441 G Street, N.W.
Washington, D.C. 20548-0001

Dear Ms. Williams-Bridgers:

We appreciate the opportunity to review your draft report, "PALESTINIAN AUTHORITY: U.S. Assistance is Training and Equipping Security Forces but the Program Needs to Measure Progress and Faces Logistical Constraints," GAO Job Code 320683.

The enclosed Department of State comments are provided for incorporation with this letter as an appendix to the final report.

If you have any questions concerning this response, please contact Steve Peterson, Program Officer, Bureau of International Narcotics and Law Enforcement Affairs at (202) 736-4376.

Sincerely,

James L. Millette

cc: GAO – David B. Gootnick
INL – David Johnson
State/OIG – Tracy Burnett

Department of State Comments on GAO Draft Report

PALESTINIAN AUTHORITY:
U.S. Assistance is Training and Equipping Security Forces but the Program Needs to Measure Progress and Faces Logistical Constraints
(GAO-10-505, GAO Code 320683)

Thank you for the opportunity to comment on your draft report entitled "PALESTINIAN AUTHORITY: U.S. Assistance is Training and Equipping Security Forces but the Program Needs to Measure Progress and Faces Logistical Constraints." Supporting the Palestinian development of the Palestinian Authority's (PA) Security Forces in accordance with the goals and objectives of the Roadmap for Peace supports the U.S. Government's foreign policy and national security priorities. It is a component in our overall effort to promote a two state solution where the Palestinian State lives side by side in peace and security with Israel. For this reason and in light of the foreign assistance funding Congress has appropriated for the Palestinian Authority Security Forces, we welcome the GAO's review of our programs and the opportunity to improve upon our efforts.

The Department of State partially concurs with the recommendation of the GAO report that the Secretary of State establish outcome-based indicators and track them over time. More specifically, that State should define specific program objectives and identify appropriate outcome-based indicators that would demonstrate progress toward achieving those objectives, and would enable it to, among other things weigh the progress made in developing the security forces, civil police, Ministry of Interior, and justice sectors. State includes performance measures and indicators for its programs, but would agree that they could be further refined. We appreciate the fact that the report acknowledges several challenges, including the still early stage of the program's development, its fluidity, and the complex political and security environment.

State recognizes the need for such indicators and has tried to develop ones that are meaningful at this stage of the program's development. For instance, every year since this program became operational in August 2007, we have included broad performance measures in the Mission Strategic Plan. INL also factors performance measures into all of its funding obligating documents: contracts with DynCorp International and DPK, amended letters of agreement with the Government of Jordan and the Palestinian Authority, and implementation letters with the Palestinian Authority. We accept GAO's point, however, that these measures should be more performance-based and now that trained and equipped security force units are in place, we anticipate developing meaningful security-related baseline data for measuring the progress of these units. We have already started to do this with our Jenin justice project, whereby the PA will be able to generate comparative data on the number, speed, and success of the cases they prosecute. In addition, INL is in the process of crafting a new Letter of Agreement (LOA) with the Palestinian Authority that will contain project goals, objectives, and milestones that reflect the program's recent and anticipated future growth in size and complexity. This LOA will replace the existing one that has been in effect since 2005, including several amendments.

We would like to caution, however, that as the report notes, there are several factors we cannot control that influence progress toward the most meaningful performance-based indicators. According to the Roadmap, "comprehensive security performance" will be measured over time by the redeployment of Palestinian security forces to areas vacated by the Israeli Defense Forces. While security assistance provided by the United States – and other donors – can strengthen the capabilities of the Palestinian security forces to operate increasingly in these areas, the Palestinian Authority will only be able to do so if it and the Government of Israel agree on the direction and pace of this deployment. Ultimately, such an agreement depends on a range of political, economic, and social factors that encompass more than just the enhanced law enforcement and security capabilities our assistance gives the PA security forces.

APPENDIX V: STAFF ACKNOWLEDGMENTS

Cheryl Goodman, Assistant Director; B. Patrick Hickey; Michael Maslowski; Jillena Roberts; Martin De Alteriis; Mary Moutsos; Reid L. Lowe; and Joseph P. Carney made key contributions to this report. Etana Finkler provided technical support.

End Notes

[1] "Performance-Based Roadmap to a Permanent Two-State Solution to the Israeli-Palestinian Conflict," (UN Document S/2003/529, May 7, 2003). Among other things, this agreement obligated the Israelis and Palestinians to undertake a series of coordinated steps to disengage Israeli troops from areas in the Palestinian territories occupied after the 2000 intifada (insurrection) and replace them with consolidated and retrained PA security forces operating under the direction of the PA Interior Minister.

[2] The Quartet is involved in mediating the peace process between the State of Israel and the PA.

[3] GAO has described how such outcome-based performance indicators can be developed and applied to program planning and management in a number of reports. GAO has also

reported that performance indicators are one of the characteristics of effective U.S. national security strategic planning and a necessary component of campaign plans created to execute those strategies. See list of related GAO products at the end of the report.

[4] The NSF is the largest uniformed service within the PASF. A battalion is made up of approximately 500 troops.

[5] State plans to build a total of nine operations camps for the 10 planned NSF battalions; State expects the 10th battalion to be deployed in other installations as a reserve force.

[6] State also allocated about $23 million for overhead items such as program design costs and the security escorts and armored vehicles State requires for U.S. government personnel to travel in the region.

[7] We have previously defined output measures as measures of an agency's products or services; outcome measures demonstrate to an external party whether the agency is achieving its intended results. See *Results-Oriented Government: GPRA Has Established a Solid Foundation for Achieving Greater Results,* GAO-04-38 (Washington, D.C.: Mar. 10, 2004).

[8] Approval process and delivery delays also constrain the efforts by other donors to provide the Presidential guard and NSF with light weapons and other lethal equipment. PA officials said the security forces lack weapons and that PA and international donor efforts to transform the security sector would be significantly hampered if these forces could not be fully armed.

[9] An additional 187,000 Israeli settlers live in the West Bank as of 2009.

[10] The Oslo Accord called for the withdrawal of Israeli forces from parts of Gaza and the West Bank and the creation of the Palestinian Interim Self-Government Authority.

[11] The first intifada refers to the Palestinian insurrection against Israeli security forces in the West Bank and Gaza between 1987 and 1993.

[12] The Tenet work plan refers to the plan to implement a cease-fire and restore security cooperation drawn up by then-Central Intelligence Agency Director George Tenet. The PA and the Government of Israel agreed to the work plan in June 2002.

[13] Hamas is a U.S. designated terrorist organization. Provisions in U.S. annual appropriations have placed restrictions on funds being provided to Hamas. The most recent provision placed restriction on funds being provided to Hamas, a Hamas-controlled entity, or any power-sharing government of which Hamas is a member, though assistance may be provided to such a power-sharing government if the President certifies that Hamas has taken certain steps such as publicly acknowledging the Jewish state of Israel's right to exist, or for national security reasons. *See* Consolidated Appropriations Act, 2010, Public Law No. 111-117, December 16, 2009. Likewise, U.S. law also places restrictions on assistance to a Hamas-controlled Palestinian Authority unless the President certifies that certain steps have been met or for national security reasons. See 22 U.S.C. § 2378b.

[14] Fatah, the secular nationalist movement formerly led by Yasser Arafat, has been the largest and dominant faction in the Palestine Liberation Organization (PLO) since 1969. The PLO recognized the right of Israel to exist in 1993. Since the establishment of the PA and limited self-rule in 1994, Fatah has dominated the PA, except for the period of Hamas participation during 2006 and 2007.

[15] USSC security assistance activities are conducted in conjunction with a broader international effort to implement PA security-sector reforms and develop government capacity. State, USAID, Canada, and other international donors provide assistance for the PA justice and penal systems, according to U.S. officials, while the European Union advises and coordinates training and other assistance for the civil police. The international community pledged $242 million at the June 2008 donor conference to support rule of law efforts and the Palestinian Civil Police through fiscal year 2011. In particular, the European Union's

Police Coordinating Office for Palestinian Police Support (EUPOL COPPS) is coordinating member nation efforts to increase the capacity of the Palestinian Civil Police with equipment donations and training support. Moreover, according to State documents, the PA Ministry of the Interior reported 16 countries and international organizations sponsored or conducted training sessions for PASF personnel between late 2008 and early 2009.

[16] In January 2009, the President appointed a Special Envoy for Middle East Peace who named the head of the USSC as his deputy for security issues. In this role the USSC head is responsible for, among other things, ensuring that U.S. security assistance efforts are effective and fully integrated with other political and economic efforts being undertaken by the U.S. government in support of the PA and peace in the region. However, the USSC formally reports through State's Near East and Asia Bureau.

[17] DOD limits the participation of U.S. military personnel in the USSC to 16, according to State and DOD officials. The Canadian Forces' Operation Proteus provides military officers in support of the USSC, including mobile observation teams deployed to the West Bank. USSC officials stated that Turkey also contributed military officers in support of the USSC.

[18] The force of 23,000 personnel represents a significant decrease from the 86,000 active and retired personnel on the PASF payroll in early 2007, according to State sources.

[19] The PASF operates under the concept of policing primacy. This is a metropolitan police concept from the United Kingdom, applied in the West Bank by the European Union to define the PASF as a national-level policing organization that has all of the capabilities, minus an army, required to deliver law and order in accordance with Roadmap security obligations for a new Palestinian state.

[20] The term "special battalion" distinguishes the new USSC-trained and -equipped units from the older NSF units these new battalions are replacing.

[21] The newly recruited battalions also receive preliminary training in the West Bank prior to their arrival in Jordan.

[22] We have reported previously on the extent to which USAID vetting procedures for its Palestinian aid program contractors complied with its antiterrorism policies, and the extent to which State and UN policies and procedures conform with U.S. statutory requirements that, among other things, no Palestinian refugee who has engaged in any act of terrorism receives funding. See GAO, *Measures to Prevent Inadvertent Payments to Terrorists under Palestinian Aid Programs Have Been Strengthened, but Some Weaknesses Remain*, GAO-09-622 (Washington, D.C.: May 19, 2009).

[23] In fiscal year 2007, INL provided $4.6 million for this training. While State budget documents note that the department allocated $2.5 million from its fiscal year 2010 budget for anti-terrorism assistance, State officials noted that they intend to reprogram those funds as they had no plans to conduct anti-terrorism activities with the PA in 2010.

[24] USSC has also funded the participation of PASF officials at a number of conferences and seminars in 2008 and 2009 on security and terrorism issues at the George C. Marshall European Center for Security Studies in Garmisch, Germany, and at the National Defense University's Near East-South Asia Center in Washington, D.C.

[25] State expects the 10th battalion to be deployed in other installations as a reserve force.

[26] The UN's Office for Project Services oversaw the initial construction. State and PA officials said they replaced this office with Palestinian contractors due to concerns about the quality of the building construction. GAO previously reported that this UN office had not assessed the effectiveness of management reforms undertaken to address key concerns raised by various audits and investigations of its operation. See *UN Office for Project Services:*

Management Reforms Proceeding but Effectiveness Not Assessed, and USAID's Oversight of Grants Has Weaknesses, GAO-10-168 (Washington, D.C.: Nov. 19, 2009).

[27] The Justice Sector Assistance Program in Jenin is designed to enhance the legitimacy and effectiveness of the PA justice sector. It seeks to build on INL's previous assistance to the PASF by improving the capacity of the Jenin justice sector, primarily the police and public prosecution, to more effectively and transparently investigate and prosecute cases.

[28] PA units initiated some security operations before they received USSC assistance. For example, the PASF initiated an ongoing effort to secure Nablus in November 2007, before the start of USSC-sponsored training.

[29] While State officials agreed that there has been a decline in the number of significant roadblocks, there is not a common agreement on the number or the definition of what constitutes a significant roadblock. Some officials stated they based this assessment on data from the government of Israel indicating the number of such roadblocks declined from 41 to 14, although the United Nations Office for Coordination of Humanitarian Affairs (OCHA) reports do not highlight this particular decline. OCHA reported that the total number of barriers (including staffed and unstaffed checkpoints, roadblocks, and mobile or other temporary barriers) rose from 561 in October 2007 to 630 in September 2008, before decreasing to 578 by October 2009. The number of staffed checkpoints (both within the West Bank and along the security barricade separating it from Israel) decreased from 93 to 69 in the same period between September 2008 and October 2009.

[30] GAO defines performance measurement as the ongoing monitoring and reporting of program accomplishments, particularly progress toward preestablished goals, and is typically conducted by program or agency management. Program measures or indicators may address, among others, the direct products and services delivered by a program (outputs), or the results of those products and services (outcomes). See GAO, *Performance Measurement and Evaluation, Definitions and Relationships,* GAO-05-739SP (Washington, D.C.: May 2005).

[31] According to a former USSC official, the PA also decided to increase the size of the NSF in part to compensate for perceived shortfalls in civil police capabilities.

[32] For example, PA officials expressed concerns about their ability to conduct effective counterterrorism efforts, and the USSC has contemplated additional counterterrorism programs in the West Bank and considered further developing specialized counterterrorism units to conduct high-risk arrests and other specialized duties. However, an Israeli official stated that his government is not in favor of the counterterrorism courses proposed by the USSC. State noted a final decision by the U.S. government on holding these courses had not yet been made as of April 2010.

[33] For example, the Palestinian Reform and Development Plan (PRDP) for 2008 through 2010, which set out basic, broad goals for Security Sector Reforms, was only adopted in 2007. The more detailed Plan for the Reorganization, Restructuring and Development of the Palestinian Security Establishment proposed in 2008 to develop the broad objectives set in the PRDP, may undergo further revision as a result of a PASF strategic review undertaken in January 2010, according to USSC officials.

[34] GAO described how such performance indicators can be developed and applied in a number of reports, including *Security Assistance: State and DOD Need to Assess How the Foreign Military Financing Program for Egypt Achieves U.S. Foreign Policy and Security Goals,* GAO-06-437 (Washington, D.C.: April 2006). See list of related GAO products at the end of the report.

[35] Previous GAO reports have noted that effective U.S. government strategies encompass certain desirable characteristics, including providing outcome-related performance measures that address priorities and milestones for progress; identify risks; and assess plans to integrate U.S., international, and host country efforts. For a full description of these characteristics, see GAO, *Rebuilding Iraq: More Comprehensive National Strategy Needed to Help Achieve U.S. Goals,* GAO-06-788 (Washington, D.C.: July 11, 2006).

[36] See DOD, Joint Publication 5-0: Joint Operation Planning (Dec. 26, 2006); and GAO, *Securing, Stabilizing, and Rebuilding Iraq Progress Report: Some Gains Made, Updated Strategy Needed,* GAO-08-837 (Washington, D.C.: June 23, 2008).

[37] GAO has highlighted the importance of establishing specific outcome-based performance measures in the development of national and multinational strategies to combat terrorism. See the list of related GAO products at the end of the report.

[38] While the mission strategic plan for fiscal year 2011 did set as a target that NSF battalions be "fully equipped and housed" in fiscal year 2010, USSC plans as of February 2010 do not reflect this as a goal.

[39] USSC and INL officials noted that other factors have also delayed the approval and delivery of equipment, including the lead times needed to redress shortfalls in manufacturers' stocks, the time needed to identify foreign vendors and obtain waivers for orders placed for items not available in the United States, and the limited availability of ships that meet program requirements that they be U.S.-flagged carriers and in compliance with Israeli port restrictions (e.g., prohibitions on the docking of ships that have visited certain Arab ports 6 months prior to arrival in Israel).

[40] An Israeli government official stated that the radios were impounded to insure their transmission frequencies do not interfere with Israeli or Jordanian frequencies. State noted that the radios remained impounded as of March 2010, even though the radios will be programmed to Government of Israel approved frequencies.

[41] State noted in some cases Israeli customs inspectors impounded approved shipments of equipment to verify whether or not some approved items were missing from the shipment.

[42] Efforts by other donors to provide the PG and NSF with light weapons and other lethal equipment have similarly been constrained by the approval process and delivery delays. For example, a USSC official noted a shipment of 1,000 AK-47 rifles approved by the Israeli government had been detained in customs. PA officials said the security forces lack weapons and that PA and international donor efforts to transform the security sector would be significantly hampered if these forces could not be fully armed. An Israeli Ministry of Defense official disputed this assertion, contending that the PASF had sufficient weapons.

[43] The Palestinian Reform and Development Plan of 2008 - 2010 created a justice-sector program, "Justice Now," which focuses on elements such as justice-sector infrastructure and capacity development.

[44] For example, according to a USSC report, the physical separation between the elements of the criminal justice sector in Jenin may form an obstacle to personal and professional cooperation, and impedes the ability of external actors to effectively monitor or assist criminal justice-sector reform.

[45] The Palestinian Legislative Council's term expired in January 2010 and no elections have yet been held to replace it. According to State officials, elections for both the President of the PA and the Legislative Council await resolution of issues concerning the scope and conduct of the elections and the eligibility of voters in Hamas-controlled Gaza to participate.

In: United States Assistance for the Palestinians ISBN: 978-1-62100-830-9
Editors: J. M. Bailey and P. F. Miller

Chapter 3

FOREIGN ASSISTANCE: UNITED STATES ASSISTANCE TO THE WEST BANK AND GAZA FOR FISCAL YEARS 2008 AND 2009*

United States Government Accountability Office

Washington, DC 20548

The Honorable Patrick J. Leahy
Chairman

The Honorable Judd Gregg
Ranking Member
Subcommittee on State, Foreign Operations,
and Related Programs
Committee on Appropriations
United States Senate

The Honorable Nita M. Lowey Chairwoman
The Honorable Kay Granger Ranking Member

---

* This is an edited, reformatted and augmented version of a United States Government Accountability Office publication, GAO-10-623R, West Bank and Gaza Funding dated May 14, 2010.

Subcommittee on State, Foreign Operations,
and Related Programs
Committee on Appropriations House of Representatives

For decades, the United States has worked toward the resolution of the Israeli-Palestinian conflict, most recently under the 2003 Roadmap for Peace, which calls for an independent Palestinian state coexisting peacefully with the State of Israel.[1] The United States had obligated more than $2.9 billion in bilateral assistance to the West Bank and Gaza focused on further developing the Palestinian economic, social services, and civil society sectors and on strengthening the processes, governance, and security-providing capacity of Palestinian Authority (PA) institutions from fiscal years 1993 through 2009. An additional $400.4 million is planned for fiscal year 2010. Since June 2007, when llamas–a U.S. designated terrorist organization–seized control of the Gaza Strip, the United States has directed most of its assistance to the West Bank.[2]

The U.S. Agency for International Development (USAID) is primarily responsible for administering Economic Support Fund (ESF) appropriations.[3] Fiscal year 2008 and 2009 ESF funds support, among other things, priority needs identified in the 2007 Palestinian Reform and Development Plan, as well as humanitarian needs in Gaza following the Israeli-llamas conflict there from December 2008 through January 2009.[4]

For fiscal years 2008 and 2009, the Congress mandated that the Comptroller General of the United States report to the Congress on U.S. assistance to the West Bank and Gaza.[5] In response to these mandates, this report (1) examines the status of USAID's obligations and expenditures[6] of the fiscal years 2008 and 2009 ESF appropriations for the West Bank and Gaza and (2) describes how the USAID mission is obligating the fiscal years 2008 and 2009 funds. In addition, in response to the mandate in the Consolidated Appropriations Act of 2008, we previously reported on the extent to which USAID has complied with its policies and procedures to help ensure that its programs do not provide support to entities or individuals associated with terrorism in the West Bank and Gaza.[7]

To address these objectives, we analyzed data provided by USAID for fiscal years 2008 and 2009 appropriations for assistance to the West Bank and Gaza as of December 31, 2009. We also met with USAID officials in Washington, D.C., and at the USAID mission (mission) in Tel Aviv, Israel, and reviewed relevant documents related to projects funded with fiscal year 2008 and fiscal year 2009 ESF funds. To determine whether the data were sufficiently reliable for purposes of this report, we requested and reviewed information from and interviewed officials at the USAID mission in Tel Aviv, Israel, about their procedures for entering contract and financial information into USAID's data system. We also requested and reviewed information from USAID officials at the Washington, D.C., headquarters about the underlying financial data system. We determined that the USAID data were sufficiently reliable for purposes of this report.

We conducted our work from July 2009 to May 2010 and in accordance with all sections of GAO's Quality Assurance Framework that are relevant to our objectives. The framework requires that we plan and perform the engagement to obtain sufficient and appropriate evidence to meet our stated objectives and to discuss any limitations in our work. We believe that the information and data we obtained, and the analysis we conducted, provide a reasonable basis for the findings in this product. (Encl. I contains a full discussion of our scope and methodology.)

SUMMARY

Of the approximately $1.17 billion in ESF assistance provided by the United States to the West Bank and Gaza from fiscal years 2008 and 2009 ESF appropriations, USAID obligated a total of about $1.16 billion and expended $678.5 million, as of December 31, 2009. More specifically, as of this date, USAID obligated 100 percent and expended over 80 percent of fiscal year 2008 ESF funds for the West Bank and Gaza.[8] For fiscal year 2009, USAID obligated approximately 98 percent and expended 47 percent of the ESF funds, as of December 31, 2009. The USAID mission in Tel Aviv reported that it plans to obligate the remaining $8.3 million in fiscal year 2009 ESF funds prior to the end of fiscal year 2010. The total of $1.17 billion in ESF funds for fiscal years 2008 and 2009 represented a large increase from previous years' appropriations, which totaled $448.7 million from fiscal years 2004 through 2007.

USAID's West Bank and Gaza mission obligated $1.15 billion in fiscal year 2008 and 2009 ESF assistance primarily for projects in five sectors: water and infrastructure, democracy and governance, health and humanitarian assistance, private enterprise, and education.[9] This assistance funds humanitarian, development, and reform projects mainly throughout the West Bank and, to a lesser extent, Gaza. Overall, USAID directed most of the fiscal year 2008 and 2009 ESF funding to the water and infrastructure sector, followed by the democracy and governance sector and health and humanitarian assistance sector. In addition, USAID also provided a total of $500 million from the $1.15 billion in obligations to the PA in three separate cash transfers for direct budgetary support. USAID officials stated that political and security conditions severely limited their ability to fund projects in Gaza in fiscal year 2008. A USAID official reported that USAID plans to commit up to $86 million in fiscal year 2009 ESF funds for humanitarian assistance and recovery projects in Gaza; however, their ability to undertake all of these planned activities is uncertain.

BACKGROUND

The Palestinian territories, comprising the West Bank and Gaza, cover 2,400 square miles and have a combined population of 4.0 million people, with over 1.5 million people in Gaza and approximately 2.5 million in the West Bank.[10] The llamas-controlled *de facto* authorities operate in Gaza while both the PA and Israel administer areas within the West Bank.[11] (See fig. 1.)

In 1993, the government of Israel and the Palestine Liberation Organization signed the Oslo Peace Accords,[12] and USAID established its West Bank and Gaza mission. In September 2000, the second *intifada* began and the Oslo peace process unraveled. Peace efforts were renewed in June 2002 when the U.S. President outlined the principles for a performance-based strategy called the Roadmap for Peace, which calls for an independent Palestinian state coexisting peacefully with the State of Israel. The United Nations, the United States, the European Union, and Russia—known as the Quartet on the Middle East[13]—as well as Israel and the PA endorsed the strategy in April 2003.

In January 2005, the Palestinian people elected Mahmoud Abbas, a supporter of the peace strategy, to be president of the PA. In January 2006, the Palestinian elections resulted in a llamas majority in the Palestinian Legislative Council. Following the results of the January 2006 election and the subsequent formation of a Fatah-llamas unity government in 2007, the Quartet on the Middle East stated that its members would continue to provide support and assistance to the llamas-led government only if the government would agree to nonviolence, recognize the State of Israel, and respect previous Israeli-Palestinian peace agreements. llamas had not met these conditions and USAID reduced and restructured its direct assistance to the Palestinians. The United States no longer provided aid directly to the PA, but instead shifted the focus of aid to providing humanitarian and project assistance indirectly through international and non-governmental organizations.[14]

Sources: GAO (data); CIA and Map Resources (map).

Figure 1. Map of West Bank and Gaza and Surrounding Countries.

In June 2007, llamas forcibly took control of the Gaza Strip. This led President Abbas to issue an emergency decree suspending the operation of the PA government and appointing a new government to administer the affairs of the West Bank during the state of emergency, under a new Prime Minister, Salam Fayyad, who is not affiliated with either llamas or Fatah. This newly formed government presented an opportunity for the United States to re-engage with the PA directly and led to increased levels of U.S. assistance aimed at improving the economic and security climate in the West Bank and increasing the capacity of the PA. In December 2007, Prime Minister Fayyad presented the Palestinian Reform and Development Plan that outlined the vision of a future Palestinian state and prioritized needs. The plan presented a private sector-led strategy for economic growth. In response to this plan, USAID has coordinated with the PA to identify a wide range of assistance activities that meet PA priority state-building needs and support a two-state solution by helping to create a peaceful and democratic Palestinian state. In August 2009, Prime Minister Fayyad released the "Program of the 13th Government: Ending the Occupation, Establishing the State," which builds on the Palestinian Reform and Development Plan and describes the PA's priorities, over a 2-year period, for establishing the necessary institutions for governing a future Palestinian state. In Gaza, according to USAID, the prohibitions on providing assistance to llamas or any entity controlled by llamas limit assistance options to programs implemented through international organizations, U.S. non-governmental organizations, and vetted local partners.

Status of U.S. Assistance to the West Bank and Gaza for Fiscal Years 2008 and 2009

In fiscal years 2008 and 2009, the United States provided a total of about $1.17 billion in ESF assistance to the West Bank and Gaza through five separate appropriations. As of December 31, 2009, USAID had obligated a total of approximately $1.16 billion of this total U.S. assistance, of which it had expended $678.5 million. (See table 1.)

Of the total fiscal year 2008 appropriations of $389 million, USAID obligated all available funds,[15] of which it expended $314.5 million, as of December 31, 2009. The Congress provided the fiscal year 2008 ESF funds through two separate appropriations.

- From the ESF funds appropriated in the 2008 Consolidated Appropriations Act, USAID was allocated $218 million for the West

Bank and Gaza.[16] Of this amount, $2 million was used for USAID administrative expenses to carry out programs in the West Bank and Gaza as allowed for in the ESF appropriations language in the act.

- From the ESF funds appropriated in the 2008 Supplemental Appropriations Act, USAID was allocated an additional $171 million for the West Bank and Gaza.[17]

Of the total fiscal year 2009 appropriations of $776 million, USAID obligated approximately $768 million, of which it expended $364 million, as of December 31, 2009. The Congress provided the fiscal year 2009 ESF funds through three separate appropriations.

- From the ESF bridge funds appropriated in the 2008 Supplemental Appropriations Act, USAID was allocated an additional $150 million in funding for the West Bank and Gaza to be made available to USAID for fiscal year 2009.[18]
- From the ESF funds appropriated in the 2009 Omnibus Appropriations Act, USAID was allocated $75 million in funding for the West Bank and Gaza.[19] As of December 31, 2009, the USAID mission had approximately $600,000 available to be obligated by the end of fiscal year 2010. USAID reported that it plans to fully obligate the remaining funds by September 30, 2010.
- From the ESF funds appropriated in the 2009 Supplemental Appropriations Act, USAID was allocated an additional $551 million in funding for the West Bank and Gaza.[20] As of December 31, 2009, approximately $7.7 million remained unobligated. USAID reported that it plans to fully obligate the remaining funds by September 30, 2010.

The combined total of about $1.17 billion for fiscal years 2008 and 2009 represented a large increase from previous years' appropriations, which totaled $448.7 million combined from fiscal years 2004 through 2007.[21] USAID directed the funding toward, among other things, supporting the PA in the West Bank and the priority reform and development needs outlined in the Palestinian Reform and Development Plan.

Table 1. Summary of Fiscal Year 2008-2009 ESF Assistance to the West Bank and Gaza as of December 31, 2009

(Millions of U.S. dollars)					
ESF appropriation	Allocated from ESF appropriation	Total obligations	Expended balance	Obligated balance	Unobligated balance
Fiscal year 2008	$389.0	$387.5	$314.5	$73.0	$0
Consolidated Appropriations Act, 2008, Pub. Law No. 110-161	218.0[b]	217.0[c]	202.4	14.6	0
Supplemental Appropriations Act, 2008, Pub. Law No. 110-252	171.0	170.5[d]	112.1	58.4	0
Fiscal year 2009	$776.0	$767.7	$364.0	$403.7	$8.3
Supplemental Appropriations Act, 2008, Pub. Law No. 110-252 (Bridge Funds)[a]	150.0	150.0	150.0	0.0	0
Omnibus Appropriations Act, 2009, Pub. Law No. 111-8	75.0	74.4[e]	12.6	61.8	0.6
Supplemental Appropriations Act, 2009, Pub. Law No. 111-32	551.0	543.3	201.4	341.9	7.7
Total	$1,165.0	$1,155.2	$678.5	$476.7	$8.3

Source: GAO analysis of USAID data.

[a] These bridge funds are ESF funds that were made available starting October 1, 2008, and remained available until September 30, 2009.

[b] Original allocation was $218.5 million; however, in response to an across-the-board rescission, USAID lowered the amount by $0.5 million to approximately $218.0 million. In addition, USAID headquarters asked the mission to convert $2 million of these funds from program to operating expense account funds to cover the administrative expenses required to carry out programs in the West Bank and Gaza, as allowed for in the appropriations act.

[c] Includes de-obligations totaling $1,001,297. According to the mission, once funds are de-obligated they do not necessarily get realloted to the mission. In this case, the funds that were de-obligated were not realloted to the mission.

[d] Includes de-obligations totaling $516,092. [e]Includes de-obligations totaling $391.

Table 2. Total Mission Obligations by ESF Appropriation Source, Fiscal Years 2008 and 2009 as of December 31, 2009

	Consolidated Appropriations Act, 2008, Pub. Law No. 110-161	Supplemental Appropriations Act, 2008, Pub. Law No. 110-252	Supplemental Appropriations Act, 2008, Pub. Law No. 110-252 (Bridge Funds)	Omnibus Appropriations Act, 2009, Pub. Law No. 111-8	Supplemental Appropriations Act, 2009, Pub. Law No. 111-32	Total 2008-2009
Development sectors						
Water and Infrastructure	$13.0	$100.3	0	$22.0	$206.4	$341.7
Democracy and Governance	12.2	28.3	0	21.0	40.0	101.5[a]
Health and Humanitarian assistance	14.8	11.2	0	11.6	59.1	96.7
Private enterprise	13.8	23.6	0	7.2	17.8	62.3
Education	7.5	0.6	0	7.7	16.3	32.1
Cash transfers/support/other						
Cash transfers	150.0	0	$150.0	0	200.0	500.0
Program support	2.9	6.6	0	4.7	0.2	14.3

Table 2. (Continued)

	Consolidated Appropriations Act, 2008, Pub. Law No. 110-161	Supplemental Appropriations Act, 2008, Pub. Law No. 110-252	Supplemental Appropriations Act, 2008, Pub. Law No. 110-252 (Bridge Funds)	Omnibus Appropriations Act, 2009, Pub. Law No. 111-8	Supplemental Appropriations Act, 2009, Pub. Law No. 111-32	Total 2008-2009
Field support/direct transfers	0.8	0	0	0.1	3.5	4.5
Total	$215.0	$170.5	$150.0	$74.4	$543.3	$1,153.2[b]

Source: GAO analysis of USAID data.

Note: Totals may differ due to rounding.

[a] A portion of the Democracy and Governance funding during these years was redirected to the emergency needs of the Gaza population following Operation Cast Lead. Of the total Democracy and Governance obligation, USAID redirected approximately $37 million to these humanitarian operations.

[b] Total does not include $2 million in operating expense account funds used to cover the administrative expenses required to carry out programs in the West Bank and Gaza.

USAID Obligations of Fiscal Year 2008 and 2009 ESF Assistance Fund Various Projects and Budgetary Support, Primarily in the West Bank

USAID's West Bank and Gaza mission obligated $1.15 billion in fiscal years 2008 and 2009 ESF funds primarily among five development sectors: water and infrastructure, democracy and governance, health and humanitarian assistance, private enterprise, and education.[22] (See table 2.) USAID also provided $500 million, from the $1.15 billion in obligations, as direct budgetary support to the PA. Most 2008 and 2009 USAID assistance is for the West Bank, as assistance to Gaza is primarily limited to humanitarian assistance.

USAID Directed Project Assistance across All Five Development Sectors in the West Bank

Through funds allocated from the fiscal years 2008 and 2009 ESF appropriations, USAID has funded various projects, primarily in the West Bank, across all five development sectors. In order to describe a cross section of these projects, we chose a project from each sector that (1) represented the largest financial obligation under that sector and (2) also received funding from at least 1 of the fiscal years 2008 and 2009 appropriations.[23]

Water and Infrastructure: The Emergency Water and Sanitation and Other Infrastructure Program

In September 2008, USAID awarded a cooperative agreement to American Near East Refugee Aid, a U.S. headquartered non-profit organization, to develop and implement the Emergency Water and Sanitation and Other Infrastructure Program. USAID estimates total costs for the program of $60 million, including $16.2 million in fiscal year 2008 and $21.7 million in fiscal year 2009 ESF funding. According to USAID documents, this program provides rapid response and emergency relief primarily in the water and sanitation sectors, and in other sectors as needed, to address the basic infrastructure needs of the Palestinian people. The program aims to rehabilitate, expand and upgrade small- and medium-scale water and sewage systems and deliver potable water to needy communities. The program will also target the construction of small-scale infrastructure to support USAID's implementation of other programs. Examples of USAID-reported accomplishments under this program include:

- Completed 18 water and sanitation projects, including laying 42,730 linear meters of water networks, installing 1,400 linear meters of rainwater drainage pipes, and providing 203,000 persons with a clean and regular supply of potable water at an affordable price.
- Completed the renovation of 141 classrooms and other educational facilities. As a result of this activity, more than 5,000 additional students will have access to improved education facilities.
- Upgraded the water and sanitation facilities of three schools to address the lack of a proper supply of potable water as well as deteriorated infrastructure.

Democracy and Governance:
Palestinian Authority Capacity Enhancement Project

In September 2008, USAID awarded a contract to Chemonics International, a large U.S. based international development consulting firm, to implement a program to support PA public sector reform efforts. USAID estimates total costs of $20 million for this project, including $10 million in fiscal year 2008 ESF funding and $6 million in 2009 ESF funding. The program assists the PA in its efforts to strengthen the operational and management capability of key ministries and public sector institutions to govern more effectively. The overall goal of the program is to create a more professional and competent public administration and civil service within the PA that provides more effective, efficient and responsive services and benefits to the Palestinian people. Activities consist of short- and medium-term capacity building, including training in areas such as leadership, communications, fiscal management, technical assistance, and the provision of equipment. Objectives of the program include the improved delivery of key services that result in immediate tangible benefits to citizens; increased financial transparency and accountability in public finance management; and strengthened public communications about, and participation in, PA decision-making. Examples of USAID-reported accomplishments under this project include:

- Conducted in-depth assessment on ways to increase revenue collection by the customs and value-added tax departments and supported a 4-week in-depth course for customs officials on classification and tariffs.

- Provided information technology and technical support to bring passport and national identification card services for over 70,000 residents in the Tubas area.
- Partially renovated the Ramallah, Hebron, and Nablus licensing bureaus to ensure more efficient and effective provision of key public services, and established a computer lab to automate driver testing and report immediate results.

Health and Humanitarian Assistance: The Palestinian Health Sector Reform and Development Project (The Flagship Project)

In September 2008, USAID awarded a contract to Chemonics International to implement the Flagship Project. USAID estimates total costs for its Flagship Project at $85 million, including obligations of $18 million in fiscal year 2008 and $27 million in fiscal year 2009 ESF funding. The Flagship Project is a 5-year initiative funded by USAID, designed in close collaboration with the Palestinian Ministry of Health. The project's main objective is to support the ministry, select nongovernmental organizations, and select educational and professional institutions in strengthening their institutional capacities and performance to support a functional, democratic Palestinian health sector able to meet its priority public health needs. The project works to achieve this goal through three components: (1) supporting health sector reform and management, (2) strengthening clinical and community-based health, and (3) supporting procurement of health and humanitarian assistance commodities. Examples of USAID-reported accomplishments under this project include:

- Supported the Ministry of Health as it conducted a health system needs assessment and finalized a 5-year Institutional Development Plan based on the results of the assessment. The plan was used as a tool to update the Ministry's National Strategic Health Plan and for donor coordination.
- Trained 354 Ministry of Health and nongovernmental organization staff on identified needs including leadership and management, health finance, costing and pricing, supervision, first responder training for ambulance drivers, advanced trauma life support, monitoring and

evaluation, procurement, community mobilization, and behavior change communications.

- Procured $703,962 worth of medical equipment and $476,157 worth of pharmaceuticals for Ministry of Health facilities and warehouses.

Private Enterprise: Expanded and Sustained Access to Financial Services Program

In September 2008, USAID awarded a cooperative agreement to the Academy for Educational Development, a U.S.-based non-profit organization, to implement a program that is to contribute to the development of a dynamic private sector in the West Bank and Gaza by improving the access of Palestinian households and small– and medium-sized businesses to financial services, especially credit, and stimulating investment in already profitable Palestinian businesses. USAID estimates total costs of the program at $36 million, including $13 million in fiscal year 2008 and $15 million in fiscal year 2009 ESF funding. The purpose of the program is to improve and expand sustainable access to financial services through the development of an efficient, inter-linked financial system and viable institutions. By assisting in the development of this system, these institutions are expected to efficiently mobilize local financial resources and provide investors with the lending facilities Palestinians need. Activities undertaken through this program include providing technical assistance and training to financial institutions to help them improve their credit management policies, business planning strategies, and lending practices; financing some capacity building needs of Palestinian credit providers, financial institutions, and relevant associations and agencies; mitigating financial risks through the development and provision of insurance products; and helping set up land and collateral registers in the West Bank and Gaza. Examples of USAID-reported accomplishments under this program include:

- Developed partnerships with 13 different institutions, facilitated $30.5 million in lending to 3,664 clients, and created 9,217 jobs.
- Assisted the Palestinian Monetary Authority, Capital Market Authority, and Ministry of National Economy with improving consumer protection regulations; developing procedures for the registration of non-bank financial institutions; building the capacity of

their staff; and reviewing, revising, and developing procedures to implement a secured transaction law.

- Helped 100 farmers build greenhouses, which led to over $100,000 in increased produce sales.

Education: The Model Schools Network Program

In September 2007, USAID awarded a cooperative agreement to American-Mideast Educational and Training Services (AMIDEAST), a U.S.-based non-profit organization, to implement the Model Schools Network Program. USAID estimates a total cost of $20 million for this program, including obligations of $2 million in fiscal year 2008 ESF and $13.2 million in fiscal year 2009 ESF funding. The Model Schools Network program will create a network of 20 private schools, which is able to design and develop educational concepts and practices for measurably improving students learning outcomes. The program focuses on four types of initiatives:

1) professional development, which focuses on the development of teachers and administrators at the model schools, particularly in the areas of English, math, and science;
2) physical capacity building, which includes computer and science lab upgrades and a small grants program providing an opportunity for member schools to apply for funds for other improvements;
3) professional networking, which includes an annual national conference, and local peer-to-peer exchanges; and
4) student and community involvement, whereby schools involved in the program actively work with parent-teacher associations and engage in an after-school youth enrichment program, and students participate in summer English, math, and science camps. Examples of USAID-reported accomplishments under this program include:

- Launched the professional certificate programs for math, science, and English classroom teachers. Ten of 16 modules were taught to approximately 140 private school teachers. In addition, all teachers received training on critical thinking and the virtual learning environment.
- Upgraded computer and science labs and procured 100 netbooks for math, science, and English teachers at the 17 private schools.
- Implemented after-school youth enrichment programs at 57 public and private schools.

USAID Provided $500 Million to the PA for Direct Budgetary Support

Out of the $1.15 billion in 2008 and 2009 ESF mission obligations, USAID provided three separate cash transfers, totaling $500 million, to the PA for direct budgetary support. According to USAID documents, given the gap between revenues and expenses for the PA, donor assistance to the PA in 2009 had been insufficient to meet its fiscal needs, falling short of PA's budgeted commitments by $30 million per month. These cash transfers were provided as follows:

- In February 2008, the President issued a waiver to allow USAID to provide $150 million in fiscal year 2008 ESF funds directly to the PA to avert an impending financial crisis.[24]
- In October 2008, the President issued another waiver to allow USAID to provide $150 million in fiscal year 2009 ESF bridge funds from the 2008 supplemental appropriation to the PA for budgetary assistance.
- In July 2009, the President issued a waiver allowing USAID to provide $200 million in fiscal year 2009 supplemental ESF funds to the PA for budget support. USAID provided this funding to meet the PA's urgent cash liquidity needs caused by larger than expected budget deficits exacerbated by the December 2008-January 2009 conflict in Gaza.

USAID's Limited Assistance to Gaza Has Focused on Humanitarian Needs

According to USAID officials, since Hamas seized control of Gaza in June 2007, USAID has directed most ESF assistance to programs in the West Bank, with programs in Gaza focused entirely on humanitarian needs. According to the USAID mission, the political and security conditions that existed in Gaza during the fiscal year 2008 implementation period severely limited their ability to support programs there, resulting in fiscal year 2008 obligations for activities in Gaza of only approximately $1.7 million. The situation in Gaza then changed in December 2008 and January 2009 with the Israeli-led Operation Cast Lead. The humanitarian crisis that developed in Gaza resulted in USAID redirecting some fiscal year 2008 funding and supplementing that with fiscal year 2009 funds to support emergency distributions of both food and non-food items. This emergency assistance committed a total of $24 million in fiscal year 2008 and 2009 ESF funds to Gaza.

Of the fiscal year 2009 funds that the mission has obligated, a mission official said USAID intends to use up to $86 million for humanitarian assistance and recovery programs in Gaza. According to mission officials, the contracts and agreements under which they have obligated these funds allow the mission to use them in either the West Bank or Gaza. However, a USAID official stated that their ability to implement that amount of funded activities in Gaza remains uncertain. The official cited difficulties in carrying out programs in Gaza including long delays in gaining Government of Israel approval for necessary shipments of materials, obstacles to staff movement in and out of Gaza, and interference with U.S. supported programs by the Hamas-led *de facto* authorities in Gaza.

Agency Comments

We provided USAID with a draft copy of this report for review and comment. USAID provided no written comments on the draft, but did provide technical comments, which we incorporated as appropriate.

David Gootnick
Director, International Affairs and Trade
Enclosures

Enclosure I: Scope and Methodology

To determine the status of appropriations, obligations, and expenditures of the Economic Support Fund (ESF) assistance to the West Bank and Gaza in fiscal years 2008 and 2009, we relied on appropriations legislation, including related conference reports, and financial data provided by USAID's West Bank and Gaza mission (the mission). The mission provided data on obligations and disbursements of all ESF funds for the West Bank and Gaza provided for in the fiscal years 2008 and 2009 annual and supplemental appropriations, as of December 31, 2009. USAID provided financial data to GAO in the form of total obligations and expenditures. For reporting purposes we converted total obligations into an obligated balance by subtracting expenditures from the total obligations reported by USAID. We also reviewed relevant USAID documents, including notifications to the Congress on the use of appropriated funds. To assess the reliability of the data provided by the mission, we requested and reviewed information from and interviewed officials at the mission about their procedures for entering contract and financial information into USAID's data system. We also requested and reviewed information from USAID officials at the Washington, D.C., headquarters about the underlying financial data system. For purposes of this report, we determined that USAID's data were sufficiently reliable.

For the project information that we include in this report, we relied on the data provided by the mission on their obligations of fiscal year 2008 and 2009 ESF funds for West Bank and Gaza. We chose projects that: (1) represented the largest financial obligation under that sector; and (2) contained obligations from one of the five fiscal year 2008 and 2009 appropriations. We reviewed the relevant agreements and accomplishment report information for each selected project. We provide project descriptions and accomplishments for illustrative purposes only. All programs selected were started in fiscal year 2008 or later. Accomplishments reported by USAID under these programs cover the period from the beginning of fiscal year 2008 through March 2010. USAID provided a summary list of major accomplishments for each selected project. From this list we provided several examples to illustrate the effects of each program. We did not independently verify the accomplishments USAID reported for the selected projects.

We conducted our work from July 2009 to May 2010 and in accordance with all sections of GAO's Quality Assurance Framework that are relevant to our objectives. The framework requires that we plan and perform the engagement to obtain sufficient and appropriate evidence to meet our stated objectives and to discuss any limitations in our work. We believe that the information and data we obtained, and the analysis we conducted, provide a reasonable basis for the findings in this product.

End Notes

[1] "A Performance-Based Roadmap to a Permanent Two-State Solution to the Israeli-Palestinian Conflict," (UN Document S/2003/529, dated May 7, 2003). Among other things, this agreement obligated the Israelis and Palestinians to undertake a series of coordinated steps to disengage Israeli troops from areas in the Palestinian territories occupied after the 2000

intifada and replace them with consolidated and retrained Palestinian Authority (PA) security forces operating under the direction of the PA Interior Minister.

[2] Provisions in U.S. annual appropriations acts have placed restrictions on funds being provided to Hamas. The most recent provision placed restrictions on funds being provided to Hamas, a Hamas controlled entity or any power sharing government of which Hamas is a member, though assistance may be provided to such a power-sharing government if the President certifies that Hamas has taken certain steps such as publicly acknowledging the Jewish state of Israel's right to exist, or for national security reasons. See Consolidated Appropriations Act, 2010, P.L. 111-117, December 16, 2009. Likewise, U.S. law also places restrictions on assistance to a Hamascontrolled Palestinian Authority unless the President certifies that certain steps have been met or for national security reasons. See 22 U.S.C. § 2378b.

[3] According to the Department of State, the ESF promotes the economic and political foreign policy interests of the United States by providing assistance to allies and countries in transition to democracy, supporting Middle East peace negotiations, and financing economic stabilization programs. Funds appropriated to the Economic Support Fund generally remain available for two years; that is, USAID would generally have two years from the time the funds were appropriated to obligate the funds. In addition, there are various restrictions placed on funds provided to the West Bank and Gaza programs in the annual appropriations acts. For example, the 2009 Omnibus Appropriations Act prohibits certain funds, including funds appropriated to the Economic Support Fund, from being used for the purpose of recognizing or otherwise honoring individuals who commit, or have committed, acts of terrorism. See Omnibus Appropriations Act, 2009, Pub. Law No. 111-8, 123 Stat. 881, Sec. 7039(c), March 11, 2009.

[4] On December 27, 2008, Israel launched a military campaign called "Operation Cast Lead" against Hamas in the Gaza Strip. The Israeli offensive came in response to markedly increased Palestinian rocket fire following the expiration of a six-month cease-fire on December 19. On January 3, 2009, Israel began a ground offensive into Gaza. Despite international pressure to halt the fighting, the conflict continued until January 18, when Israel unilaterally ceased fire. Hamas ceased fire shortly thereafter.

[5] Consolidated Appropriations Act, 2008, Pub. Law No. 110-161, Sec. 657(e)(2), Dec. 26, 2007 and Omnibus Appropriations Act, 2009, Pub. Law No. 111-08, Sec. 7039(e)(2), March 11, 2009.

[6] For this report, we use the term "expenditures" to mean cash disbursements.

[7] GAO, *Foreign Assistance: Measures to Prevent Inadvertent Payments to Terrorists under Palestinian Aid Programs Have Been Strengthened, but Some Weaknesses Remain,* GAO-09-622 (Washington, D.C.: May 19, 2009).

[8] Approximately $1.5 million in fiscal year 2008 obligations were later de-obligated and not re-allotted to the mission.

[9] USAID obligated $18.8 million, from the $1.15 billion in 2008 and 2009 ESF fund obligations, for program and field support activities and direct transfers.

[10] Central Intelligence Agency World Factbook.

[11] In June 2007, fighting between the two major political parties within the PA, Fatah and Hamas, resulted in Hamas forcibly seizing control of the Gaza Strip, creating a Hamas-led de facto government in Gaza.

[12] The accords called for the withdrawal of Israeli forces from parts of the Gaza Strip and West Bank and affirmed the Palestinian right to self-government within those areas through the creation of the Palestinian Interim Self Government Authority. Palestinian rule would last for a 5-year interim period during which a permanent agreement would be negotiated.

[13] The Quartet is involved in mediating the peace process between the State of Israel and the PA.

[14] GAO previously reported on changes to U.S. aid to the Palestinians as a result of the January 2006 elections. See *Foreign Assistance: U.S. Assistance to the West Bank and Gaza for Fiscal Years 2005 and 2006*, GAO-07-443R (Washington, D.C.: Mar. 5, 2007).

[15] Obligations of fiscal year 2008 ESF funds totaled $387.5 million; however, this does not include roughly $1.5 million in deobligations of previously obligated 2008 ESF funds that were not realloted to the mission.

[16] Consolidated Appropriations Act, 2008, Pub. Law No. 110-161, December 26, 2007. Originally, Congress had appropriated not more than $218.5 million in ESF funding for the West Bank and Gaza. However, in response to an across-the-board rescission, USAID lowered the amount by $0.5 million to approximately $218.0 million.. See Section 699P of Division J of the Consolidated Appropriations Act, 2008, Pub. Law No. 110-161, Dec. 26, 2007.

[17] Supplemental Appropriations Act, 2008, Pub. Law No. 110-252, June 30, 2008.

[18] Supplemental Appropriations Act, 2008, Pub. Law No. 110-252, June 30, 2008.

[19] Omnibus Appropriations Act of 2009, Pub. Law No. 111-8, March 11, 2009

[20] Supplemental Appropriations Act, 2009, Pub. Law No. 111-32, June 24, 2009.

[21] As a result of carry-over funds from previous years, mission obligations from fiscal years 2004 through 2007 totaled $725 million.

[22] USAID obligated $18.8 million of 2008 and 2009 ESF funds for program and field support activities and direct transfers.

[23] All contracts selected began in fiscal year 2008 or later. USAID-reported accomplishments under these contracts cover the period from the beginning of fiscal year 2008 through March 2010. We did not independently verify the accomplishments USAID reported for the selected projects.

[24] Consistent with language in the 2008 Consolidated Appropriations Act, before more than $100,000,000 of ESF funds were made available for cash transfer assistance to the PA, the Secretary of State certified and reported to the Committees on Appropriations that the PA had (1) established a single treasury account for all PA financing and all financing mechanisms flow through this account, (2) eliminated all parallel financing mechanisms outside of the PA treasury account, and (3) established a single comprehensive civil service roster and payroll. *See* Pub. Law No. 110-161, 121 Stat. 2298, Dec. 26, 2007.

In: United States Assistance for the Palestinians ISBN: 978-1-62100-830-9
Editors: J. M. Bailey and P. F. Miller

Chapter 4

FOREIGN ASSISTANCE: MEASURES TO PREVENT INADVERTENT PAYMENTS TO TERRORISTS UNDER PALESTINIAN AID PROGRAMS HAVE BEEN STRENGTHENED, BUT SOME WEAKNESSES REMAIN*

United States Government Accountability Office

WHY GAO DID THIS STUDY

The U.S. government is one of the largest donors to Palestinians. It provided nearly $575 million in assistance in fiscal year 2008. This assistance is provided through the U.S. Agency for International Development (USAID) and through contributions to international organizations, primarily the United Nations Relief and Works Agency for Palestine Refugees in the Near East (UNRWA). The Department of State (State) oversees U.S. contributions to UNRWA. To help ensure that U.S. funds for these programs are not provided to individuals or entities engaged in terrorist activities, USAID and State must comply with restrictions under U.S. law. GAO was asked to (1) assess the extent to which USAID has complied with its antiterrorism policies and

* This is an edited, reformatted and augmented version of the United States Government Accountability Office publication, Report to Congressional Committees, GAO-09-622, dated May 2009.

procedures and (2) assess State's and UNRWA's policies and procedures to support conformance with U.S. statutory conditions. GAO reviewed U.S. and UNRWA documents; interviewed USAID, State, and UNRWA officials; and conducted fieldwork in Israel, Jerusalem, and Jordan.

WHAT GAO RECOMMENDS

To strengthen compliance, GAO recommends that the Administrator of USAID improve monitoring of subawards. GAO also recommends that the Secretary of State consider taking additional steps to oversee UNRWA's conformance with U.S. conditions on funding. USAID, State, and UNRWA said they are taking actions to implement GAO's recommendations.

WHAT GAO FOUND

USAID strengthened its antiterrorism policies and procedures and complied with them in making new prime awards, but had weaknesses related to compliance at the subaward level. ("Prime awardee" refers to an organization that directly receives USAID funding to implement projects. "Subawardee" refers to an organization that receives funding from prime awardees.) USAID strengthened its policies and procedures in response to our 2006 recommendations by, for example, strengthening its vetting process, which involves investigating a person or entity for links to terrorism. Since 2006, USAID has instituted new procedures to monitor prime awardee compliance with antiterrorism requirements, which have allowed it to take some actions to address areas of concern. The agency has hired a specialist who reviews prime awardees' subaward files for compliance with its antiterrorism policies. All 32 new prime awards made by USAID in fiscal year 2008 included all applicable clauses. USAID obtained the applicable antiterrorism certifications and conducted required vetting for all applicable new prime awards. For a random sample of fiscal year 2008 subawards, applicable antiterrorism certifications were obtained and vetting was conducted. However, an estimated 17 percent of subawards had insufficient evidence to assess compliance related to mandatory clauses. For the remaining subawards, an estimated 5 percent did not contain the mandatory clauses at the time of the award. GAO also found limitations in the agency's monitoring of subawards for inclusion of mandatory clauses.

Since 2003, State and UNRWA have strengthened policies and procedures to conform with conditions on U.S. contributions to UNRWA, but weaknesses remain. Section 30 1(c) of the Foreign Assistance Act of 1961, as amended, prohibits U.S. contributions to UNRWA except on the condition that UNRWA take all possible measures to assure that no part of the U.S. contribution shall be used to furnish assistance to, among others, any refugee who has engaged in any act of terrorism. UNRWA has agreed to conform to conditions on U.S. contributions, but State has not established criteria to determine whether UNRWA's actions are consistent with this agreement. While State has not defined the key term "all possible measures" or defined nonconformance, it has strengthened some policies and procedures to oversee UNRWA's conformance. UNRWA has strengthened policies and procedures to promote neutrality of its beneficiaries, staff, contractors, and facilities that cover a broader range of conduct than covered in section 301(c). UNRWA reported denying approximately 110 applications for cash assistance to refugees since July 2006, because the agency found the refugees' behavior was inconsistent with UN neutrality or restrictions related to section 30 1(c). However, limitations exist. UNRWA said it has screened all staff, contractor, and beneficiary names against a UN Security Council list of potential terrorists and found no matches. However, the list does not include Hamas and Hezbollah, which the United States has designated as foreign terrorist organizations. Finally, internal UNRWA audits do not assess controls for all cash assistance programs or whether contracts contain antiterrorism clauses.

ABBREVIATIONS

OFAC	U.S. Department of Treasury's Office of Foreign Assets Control
OSO	Operation Support Officer
PRM	State Department Bureau of Population, Refugees and Migration
PSU	Program Support Unit
PVS	Partner Vetting System
State	U.S. Department of State
the mission	USAID Mission to the West Bank and Gaza
UN	United Nations

UN	1267 list Al-Qaida and Taliban Sanctions Committee Consolidated List
UNRWA	United Nations Relief and Works Agency for Palestine Refugees in the Near East
USAID	U.S. Agency for International Development

May 19, 2009
Congressional Committees

For decades, the United States has played a leading role in efforts to resolve the Israeli-Palestinian conflict. Since 1948, Palestinians in the West Bank, Gaza, and neighboring countries have received education, economic revitalization, health services, and infrastructure assistance. The U.S. government is one of the largest donors to Palestinians. It provided nearly $575 million in assistance in fiscal year 2008. This assistance is mainly provided bilaterally, through the U.S. Agency for International Development (USAID), and multilaterally, through contributions to international organizations, primarily the United Nations Relief and Works Agency for Palestine Refugees in the Near East (UNRWA). The Department of State (State) oversees U.S. contributions to UNRWA. The bilateral and multilateral aid programs differ substantially in their methods of providing assistance. For example, while USAID relies heavily on contractors[1] to implement projects that improve the welfare of Palestinians, such as building water distribution networks, UNRWA hires nearly 30,000 employees to directly provide social and humanitarian services, such as education and health care. To help ensure that U.S. funds for these programs are not provided to individuals or entities engaged in terrorist activities, USAID and State must comply with restrictions under U.S. law when providing funds for Palestinian assistance programs.

The Consolidated Appropriations Act of 2008[2] directs the Comptroller General to conduct an audit and an investigation of the treatment, handling, and uses of all funds for the bilateral West Bank and Gaza Program in fiscal year 2008 under the Economic Support Fund, including an assessment of the extent to which this program has complied with the requirements attached to these funds in this legislation.[3] In addition, House Report 110-197[4] directs GAO to assess UNRWA's complianc e with conditions required by law on U.S. contributions to UNRWA, particularly UNRWA's cash assistance program. In response to previous mandates, we assessed UNRWA's actions to implement section 301(c) of the Foreign Assistance Act of 1961, as amended, in 2003 [5] and USAID's compliance in 2006.[6] We made no recommendations in our 2003 report. USAID implemented four recommendations from our 2006 report, which were intended to strengthen USAID efforts to help ensure that U.S. assistance to the West Bank and Gaza does not support terrorist activities. For example, as we recommended, USAID clarified how its antiterrorism policies and procedures would be applied to certain types of assistance instruments.

In response to the appropriations act and the House report, as well as a request from the House Foreign Affairs Committee and its Subcommittee on the Middle East and South Asia, we (1) assessed the extent to which USAID has complied with its policies and procedures to help ensure that its programs do not provide support to entities or individuals associated with terrorism in the West Bank and Gaza, and (2) assessed State's and UNRWA's policies and procedures to support conformance with U.S. statutory conditions placed on contributions provided to UNRWA to prohibit funding of terrorist-related activities.

To address the first objective, we analyzed key documents and data provided by USAID and interviewed USAID and prime awardee officials in Jerusalem, Tel Aviv, and Washington, D.C. We also analyzed (1) all 32 new prime awards made by USAID in fiscal year 2008 using Economic Support Funds and (2) a random sample of 144 out of 2,620 subaward agreements that USAID identified for us as made by prime awardees in fiscal year 2008. We assessed both prime awards and subawards against the requirements stipulated by USAID to help ensure compliance with U.S. legal requirements prohibiting support for terrorist-related activities. To address the second objective, we analyzed key documents and data provided by State and UNRWA; interviewed State officials in Jerusalem and Washington, D.C.; interviewed UNRWA officials; and observed UNRWA programs in Jordan and the West Bank.

We conducted this performance audit from August 2008 to May 2009 in accordance with generally accepted government auditing standards. Those standards require that we plan and perform the audit to obtain sufficient, appropriate evidence to provide a reasonable basis for our findings and conclusions based on our audit objectives. We believe that the evidence obtained provides a reasonable basis for our findings and conclusions based on our audit objectives. (App. I provides a detailed discussion of our objectives, scope, and methodology.)

RESULTS IN BRIEF

We found that USAID strengthened its antiterrorism policies and procedures and complied with them when making new prime awards, but had weaknesses related to compliance at the subaward level. In response to our 2006 recommendation, USAID strengthened its antiterrorism policies and procedures by clarifying how each would apply to certain types of assistance instruments and by strengthening its vetting process, which involves investigating a person or entity for links to terrorism. Since our 2006 report, USAID has also instituted new procedures to monitor prime awardee compliance with antiterrorism requirements, which have allowed it to identify and take some actions to address areas of concern we found. For example, the agency has hired a compliance specialist who reviews prime awardees' subaward files for compliance with its antiterrorism policies. All 32 new prime awards made by USAID in fiscal year 2008 included all applicable clauses. In addition, USAID obtained the antiterrorism certifications, where applicable, and conducted required vetting for all applicable new prime awards. We also found that USAID vetted all the appropriate officials, when required, for our sampled subawards. For our random sample of 144 fiscal year 2008 subawards, applicable antiterrorism certifications were obtained and vetting was conducted. However, regarding mandatory clauses, we estimated that insufficient evidence exists to assess compliance for approximately 17 percent of the fiscal year 2008 subawards USAID identified. For the estimated 83 percent of subawards with sufficient evidence to assess compliance, we estimated that approximately 5 percent had weaknesses related to the inclusion of mandatory clauses while the remaining 95 percent did not. We also found limitations in how the agency monitors prime awardee compliance with requirements related to the inclusion of mandatory clauses in subawards.

Since our 2003 report, State and UNRWA have strengthened policies and procedures to conform with conditions on U.S. contributions to UNRWA, but weaknesses remain. Section 30 1(c) of the Foreign Assistance Act of 1961, as amended, prohibits U.S. contributions to UNRWA except on the condition that UNRWA take all possible measures to assure that no part of the U.S. contribution shall be used to furnish assistance to, among others, any refugee who has engaged in any act of terrorism. While UNRWA has agreed to conform to conditions on U.S. contributions, State has not established criteria to determine whether UNRWA's actions are consistent with this agreement. For example, State has not defined the key term "all possible measures" or defined what would constitute nonconformance. Nevertheless, State has strengthened some policies and procedures to oversee UNRWA's conformance with conditions on U.S. contributions. UNRWA has also implemented and strengthened policies and procedures to promote neutrality of its beneficiaries, staff, contractors, and facilities that cover a broader range of conduct than covered in section 301(c). UNRWA reported denying approximately 110 applications for discretionary cash assistance to refugees since July 2006, because the agency found the refugees' behavior was inconsistent with UN neutrality or restrictions related to section 30 1(c). However, we found limitations in some of UNRWA's efforts. For example, UNRWA told us it has screened all staff, contractor, and beneficiary names against a UN Security Council list of potential terrorists and found no matches. However, the list is restricted to individuals and entities affiliated with Al-Qaida and the Taliban and thus does not specifically include major regional groups, such as Hamas and Hezbollah, which the United States has designated as foreign terrorist organizations. Finally, we found that internal audits of UNRWA do not assess whether contracts contain required antiterrorism clauses or assess controls for UNRWA's overall cash assistance program.

To strengthen compliance with USAID policies and procedures at the subaward level, we recommend that the Administrator of USAID take action to help ensure that prime awardees comply with USAID requirements to include mandatory clauses in subawards. In addition, to help ensure that assistance is not inadvertently provided to terrorists, we recommend that the Secretary of State consider taking additional steps to oversee UNRWA's conformance with U.S. conditions on funding, such as (1) establishing criteria to evaluate UNRWA's efforts; (2) screening the names of UNRWA contractors against lists of individuals and entities of concern to the United States; and (3) monitoring UNRWA's commitment that future internal audits would assess UNR WA's compliance with its neutrality and antiterrorism policies for contractors as well as internal controls for cash assistance.

USAID, State, and UNRWA provided written comments on a draft of this report, which are reprinted in appendices IV, V, and VI. USAID, State, and UNRWA outlined actions they intend to take to implement our recommendations. USAID stated that our work contributed positively to the continuous improvement and strengthening of USAID West Bank and Gaza mission's compliance with antiterrorism policies and procedures. However, USAID disagreed with our finding that insufficient evidence was present to assess a significant percentage of fiscal year 2008 subawards. We maintain that evidence was insufficient because the only references to the purchase orders that were included on the mandatory clauses were individual handwritten annotations. It was not clear who made the annotations and when those annotations were made. State is undertaking actions to address all three parts of our recommendation, but noted that it will need to address the resource implications of two of these. State expressed some concern about the resources required to undertake effective screening and noted that conducting additional internal audits would result in additional costs to UNRWA. UNRWA made a commitment that future internal UNRWA audits would assess the agency's compliance with its neutrality and antiterrorism policies for contractors and internal controls for cash assistance.

Background

The U.S. government has provided assistance to Palestinians both bilaterally and multilaterally for several decades. USAID is the agency primarily responsible for implementing the bilateral aid program, while State oversees annual contributions to international organizations, primarily to UNRWA, for the multilateral program. The focus, size, and intent of the bilateral and multilateral programs differ. Table 1 compares the main characteristics of the two programs.

To help ensure that U.S. funds for these programs are not provided to individuals or entities engaged in terrorist activities, State and USAID must comply with restrictions under U.S. law when providing funds for Palestinian assistance programs. For the bilateral aid program, section 657(b) of the Consolidated Appropriations Act of 2008 states the following:

> "Prior to the obligation of funds appropriated by this Act under the heading 'Economic Support Fund' for assistance for the West Bank and Gaza, the Secretary of State shall take all appropriate steps to ensure that such assistance is not provided to or through any individual, private or government entity, or educational institution that the Secretary knows or has reason to believe advocates, plans, sponsors, engages in, or has engaged in, terrorist activity nor, with respect to private entities or educational institutions, those that have as a principal officer of the entity's governing board or governing board of trustees any individual that has been determined to be involved in, or advocating terrorist activity or determined to be a member of a designated foreign terrorist organization. The Secretary of State shall, as appropriate, establish procedures specifying the steps to be taken in carrying out this subsection and shall terminate assistance to any individual, entity, or educational

institution which she has determined to be involved in or advocating terrorist activity."

In addition, the act states:

> "None of the funds appropriated under title II through V of this Act for assistance under the West Bank and Gaza program may be made available for the purpose of recognizing or otherwise honoring individuals who commit, or have committed, acts of terrorism."[7]

The Secretary of State has deferred to USAID, the implementing agency, to ensure compliance with these and similar provisions. The USAID Mission to the West Bank and Gaza (the mission) developed Mission Order 21, which outlines USAID's procedures to help ensure that its assistance program does not inadvertently provide support to entities or individuals associated with terrorism, in accordance with U.S. law.[8] Mission Order 21 establishes, among others, the following requirements:

- All solicitations and awards for contracts, grants, and subagreements must contain the *antiterrorism clause.* This clause reminds award recipients that they must comply with U.S. executive orders and laws prohibiting transactions with terrorists, and the provision of resources and support to individuals or organizations associated with terrorism. UN agencies that receive USAID funds must include a separate clause.
- All U.S. and non-U.S. organizations must sign the *antiterrorism certification* before being awarded a grant or cooperative agreement to certify that the organization does not provide material support or resources for terrorism. This certification recommends that the recipient follow certain steps to comply with its obligation, including (1) screening against the U.S. Department of Treasury's Office of Foreign Assets Control (OFAC) list[9] and the UN Security Council's Al-Qaida and Taliban Sanctions Committee Consolidated List (UN 1267 list)[10] before providing any material support or resources to an individual or entity and (2) implementing reasonable monitoring and oversight procedures to safeguard against assistance being diverted to support terrorist activity.

Table 1. Key Features of USAID and UNRWA Programs for Assistance to Palestinians

	USAID	UNRWA
Fiscal year 2008 U.S. funding	$389.5 million appropriated in Economic Support Funds to provide assistance to the West Bank and Gaza. This includes about $900,000 that was obligated to the World Food Program to provide food for families in Gaza.	State contributed about $185 million to UNRWA—nearly $171 million from the Migration and Refugee Assistance account and $14 million from the Emergency Refugee and Migration Assistance Fund.
Focus of program	Strengthens Palestinian institutions and invests in projects that improve the health and welfare of the Palestinian people. Projects include funds to • provide technical assistance to Palestinian health institutions, • improve water infrastructure in the West Bank, and • provide immediate employment opportunities through the construction of small-scale infrastructure. Provided over $3.3 million in cash assistance to about 6,000 recipients, mainly for scholarships and tuition, in fiscal year 2008, according to USAID estimates.	Directly provides social services and humanitarian support to Palestinian refugees. UNRWA's 2008 program budget was allocated as follows: • 52 percent for education services, • 19 percent for health, • 13 percent for support services, • 9 percent for relief and social services, • 5 percent for infrastructure and camp improvement, and • 2 percent for microfinance and microenterprise. UNRWA reported it spent $88.8 million for cash assistance to refugees from January 2006 through December 2008—$36.2 million for cash subsidies for food and selective cash assistance from its General Fund and $52.6 million in emergency cash assistance from its Emergency Appeal.
Program Implementation	Contractors and grantees implement programs.	UNRWA directly implements most programs and relies minimally on contractors to provide supplies and equipment. The majority of UNRWA staff are directly involved in providing services, for example, as doctors, teachers, social workers or sanitation laborers. Staff costs account for much of the agency's regular budget

	USAID	UNRWA
Location and size of organization	USAID Mission to the West Bank and Gaza (the mission), located in Tel Aviv, Israel, manages programs. According to USAID officials, the mission is staffed by 137 individuals including Foreign Service Nationals.	UNRWA headquarters are in Gaza and Amman, Jordan. UNRWA employs nearly 30,000 staff. About 90 percent of these staff are locally-recruited Palestinian refugees. UNRWA also employs 183 international staff.
Location and funding of projects and services	Mainly the West Bank; USAID used only a small percentage of funds for assistance activities in Gaza.	UNRWA's 2008 to 2009 regular budget for operations was allocated among field offices as follows: • 31 percent in Gaza • 22 percent in Jordan • 17 percent in the West Bank • 13 percent in Lebanon • 9 percent in Syria • 8 percent in UNRWA headquarters, Amman and Gaza

Source: GAO analysis of USAID and UNRWA documents and estimated funding amounts for cash assistance.

Notes: UNRWA has two primary sources of funding: (1) the General Fund, which is funded through voluntary contributions to UNRWA's regular budget annually, and (2) the Emergency Appeal, which is funded through an appeal by UNRWA's Commissioner-General to donors for emergency funding in response to a crisis in a particular UNRWA field area of operations. The United States does not currently limit contributions to UNRWA's General Fund to specific purposes. However, as of July 2007, State said it placed limitations on all its contributions to UNRWA's Emergency Appeal for West Bank and Gaza so that no U.S. funds are to be used for UNRWA's emergency cash assistance activities in West Bank and Gaza.

According to the mission, none of the scholarship or tuition funds were provided to the recipients. All assistance was provided directly to the relevant school on their behalf.

- All contracts, subcontracts, grants, cooperative agreements, and subgrants must contain the clause restricting facility names, known as the *naming clause*. This clause states, among other things, that no assistance shall be provided under this contract or agreement for any school, community center or other facility that is named after any person or group that has advocated, sponsored, or committed acts of terrorism.
- Certain individuals and organizations need to be *vetted*, which involves checking recipients' names and other identifying information against databases and other information sources to determine if they have links to terrorism.

For UNRWA, section 301(c) of the Foreign Assistance Act of 1961, as amended, states the following:

> "No contributions by the United States shall be made to the United Nations Relief and Works Agency for Palestinian Refugees in the Near East except on the condition that the United Nations Relief and Works Agency takes all possible measures to assure that no part of the United States contribution shall be used to furnish assistance to any refugee who is receiving military training as a member of the so-called Palestinian Liberation Army or any other guerrilla type organization or who has engaged in any act of terrorism."[11]

This clause is commonly referred to as "section 301(c)."

State is responsible for implementing section 30 1(c) and, in that capacity, oversees U.S. contributions to UNRWA. UNRWA beneficiaries include Palestinian refugees and a limited number of individuals displaced by the 1967 Arab-Israel conflict. According to UNRWA, most of the displaced individuals are in Jordan.

UNRWA's Beneficiaries

UNRWA's beneficiaries include 4.6 million individuals who have registered with UNRWA for refugee status. Under UNRWA's operational definition, Palestinian refugees are individuals

- whose normal place of residence was Palestine between June 1946 and May 1948,

- who lost both their homes and means of livelihood as a result of the 1948 Arab- Israeli conflict, or
- who are descendants through the male line of individuals who became refugees in 1948.

UNRWA also provides health and education services to individuals displaced by the 1967 Arab-Israeli conflict.

USAID Strengthened Its Antiterrorism Policies and Procedures and Complied with Them in Making New Prime Awards, but Has Weaknesses in Compliance at the Subaward Level

Since 2006, USAID has strengthened its antiterrorism policies and procedures to help ensure that assistance is not inadvertently provided to terrorists. USAID complied with its strengthened policies and procedures when issuing new prime awards in fiscal year 2008. Although USAID's new monthly reporting system was intended, in part, to improve compliance at the subaward level, we found that it did not provide sufficient information for us to assess compliance.

USAID Strengthened Its Antiterrorism Policies and Procedures

USAID Strengthened Its Antiterrorism Policies and Procedures by Clarifying How They Apply to Each Assistance Agreement

In response to our 2006 recommendation, USAID strengthened its antiterrorism policies and procedures—as outlined in Mission Order 21— to help ensure that assistance is not inadvertently provided to terrorists by clarifying how those policies and procedures would be applied to each type of assistance instrument. Although USAID had established antiterrorism provisions that apply to contracts, cooperative agreements, and grants, we reported in 2006 that it had not clearly articulated how antiterrorism provisions apply to other types of assistance instruments, such as purchase orders.[12] We recommended that USAID develop policies and procedures to address how each of its antiterrorism provisions apply to other types of assistance instruments. In its October 3, 2007, revision to Mission Order 21, USAID strengthened its antiterrorism policies and procedures by listing which clauses and certifications would apply to each type of assistance instrument—thereby responding to our 2006 recommendation. For example, the antiterrorism certification now clearly applies to grants made under contracts. In addition, USAID clarified that instruments that can function as contracts, such as purchase orders, are subject to the same policies as contracts.

USAID Strengthened Its Vetting Process

USAID strengthened its vetting process in response to a 2006 GAO recommendation that the mission's vetting management database promote data reliability, satisfy technical documentation requirements, and meet all applicable security requirements. This recommendation was based on our finding that the mission did not routinely collect or verify detailed identifying information—such as date and place of birth—needed to fully vet individuals. We also identified weaknesses in the mission's unclassified database, which was designed to record and track vetting results. For example, few safeguards were in place to control access to the information stored in the database. In response to our recommendation and findings, the following were completed:

- In December 2006, USAID instituted a new strengthened vetting system, called the Partner Vetting System. This system uses U.S. law enforcement and intelligence databases to vet the names of individuals that it receives from the mission. It also requires additional information for individuals being screened, such as the individual's government-issued photo identification number and type (e.g., passport and passport number). Access to the system is limited to certain individuals who may have different levels of access to information in the system. For example, the clerks who enter vetting information do not have the same level of access as the contracting officer who makes the award.
- USAID placed a U.S. citizen with a security clearance in charge of the office responsible for maintaining the vetting system, thereby enabling sensitive derogatory information on potential awardees to be shared with the mission. Derogatory information indicates that vetted organizations or individuals appear to have links with terrorism.

- USAID conducted additional vetting at the U.S. consulate in Jerusalem for organizations receiving cash or in-kind assistance, which serves as another review to help ensure that funds are not inadvertently given to terrorists.

According to USAID officials and prime awardees we spoke with, these improvements have strengthened controls over the system and decreased vetting time from about 9 months to as little as 1 to 2 weeks.

USAID Enhanced Monitoring Efforts to Provide More Timely Information on Compliance

In 2008, USAID enhanced its efforts to monitor prime awardee compliance with applicable Mission Order 21 requirements by commissioning an additional compliance audit, hiring a compliance specialist to conduct recurring compliance reviews, and requiring that prime awardees address noncompliance findings. USAID commissioned an additional compliance audit by contracting with an independent auditing firm to review 15 prime awardees' compliance with Mission Order 21 during the period from June 1, 2006, through January 31, 2008. The audits examined 1,094 subawards and found 70 total weaknesses; 62 awards contained at least 1 weakness and 5 of those awards contained multiple weaknesses. Thirty-eight of the 70 weaknesses were related to mandatory clauses, 13 were related to vetting approval, and 4 were related to vetting procedures. The audit also found 15 monthly reporting weaknesses. According to USAID officials, where appropriate, prime awardees took actions to address the identified weaknesses. They also said that, in response to these findings, mandatory clauses were inserted into subawards when necessary, and required vetting was conducted and each subawardee passed vetting. This one-time audit provided additional feedback to USAID on the 15 prime awardees' compliance beyond the existing feedback provided through the annual Regional Inspector General audits.[13]

Building on the one-time additional compliance audit, USAID further enhanced its oversight of prime awardees' efforts to comply with their Mission Order 21-related requirements by hiring, in 2008, a compliance specialist. This specialist is responsible for conducting recurring compliance reviews of prime awardees' subaward activities. Previously, USAID only examined prime awardee compliance with these requirements as part of periodic contract and compliance audits conducted under the direction of the Regional Inspector General. According to USAID officials, the compliance specialist's reviews allow USAID to monitor compliance on a more timely basis than can be done with the annual USAID Regional Inspector General audits. In July 2008 the compliance specialist began conducting periodic site visits to prime awardee locations to review records related to the subawards made under USAID contracts and assistance agreements to determine whether they complied with Mission Order 21. According to the mission, the compliance specialist's review includes inspecting documents related to each subaward contract or agreement to confirm that (1) the prime awardee had received evidence from USAID that required preaward vetting had occurred and the subawardee was eligible; (2) each subaward contract or agreement had related mandatory clauses; and (3) where applicable, the prime awardee had obtained from subawardees a signed and dated antiterrorism certification prior to making the subaward. In addition, the mission stated that, whenever possible, the compliance specialist reviews the prime awardees' records of subaward activity to determine whether all required subawards were included in the monthly subaward reports. The compliance specialist uses a standardized checklist to determine whether an award is compliant with Mission Order 21.

The compliance specialist found problems with some prime awardees' compliance with Mission Order 21 and their monthly reports, most of which, according to the mission, have been resolved. In his first draft summary report, the compliance specialist reviewed 2,883 subawards issued by 32 prime awardees for compliance with Mission Order 21. The specialist discovered 26 instances where the subaward did not include the naming clause, 13 where the subaward did not include the antiterrorism clause, and 2 where the antiterrorism certification was not signed prior to the award being made. The compliance specialist also found 5 instances of noncompliance with Mission Order 21's vetting policies. In one of those instances, for example, USAID disallowed the costs submitted by the prime awardee because the prime awardee issued the subaward without obtaining vetting approval. The mission said the subawardees were subsequently vetted and cleared in the remaining four cases. According to the mission, awardees have since resolved most instances of noncompliance found by the reviewer. The remaining instances were not corrected because the award had already expired or had been cancelled by the prime awardee. Additionally, the compliance specialist found 66 instances where prime awardees had not correctly reported their subawards in their monthly reports to USAID.

USAID Complied with Its Strengthened Antiterrorism Policies and Procedures at the Prime Award Level

USAID Included All Applicable Clauses in All New Prime Awards Made in Fiscal Year 2008 and Obtained Required Certifications

Mission Order 21 requires the USAID Mission to vet the following:

- All prime awardee and subawardee nonU.S. organizations or individuals (16 years old or older) proposed for a contract or subcontract above $25,000.
- All prime awardee and subawardee nonU.S. organizations or individuals (16 years old or older) proposed to receive cash or in-kind assistance under a cooperative agreement, grant, or subgrant.
- All non-U.S. individuals (16 years old or older) who receive USAID-financed training, study tours or invitational travel in the United States or third countries or who receive training in the West Bank/Gaza lasting more than 5 consecutive work days.
- All entities or specifically identified persons (16 years old or older) who directly receive other forms of cash or in-kind assistance, with the following exceptions (these thresholds apply to a single award and are not cumulative):

- individuals who receive jobs under employment generation activities,
- individuals who receive assistance of $1,000 or less,
- organizations that receive assistance of $2,500 or less,
- households that receive micro- enterprise loans or assistance of $5,000 or less, and
- vendors of goods or services acquired by USAID contractors and grantees in the ordinary course of business for their own use.

Even if vetting would not otherwise be required under these rules, vetting will be conducted whenever there is reason to believe that the beneficiary of assistance or the vendor of goods or services commits, attempts to commit, advocates, facilitates, or participates in terrorist acts, or has done so in the past.

We found that all 32 new prime awards made by USAID in fiscal year 2008 contained the appropriate mandatory clauses—the antiterrorism and naming clauses—and, where applicable, USAID had obtained the advanced antiterrorism certifications,[14] as required under Mission Order 21. The antiterrorism clause reminds award recipients that they must comply with U.S. executive orders and laws prohibiting transactions with terrorists and the provision of resources and support to individuals or organizations associated with terrorism. The naming clause states that no assistance shall be provided under this contract or agreement for any school, community center, or other facility that is named after any person or group that has advocated, sponsored, or committed acts of terrorism.[15] USAID officials said there are relatively few situations where the United States is providing assistance to the West Bank and Gaza that involves naming buildings or structures. The antiterrorism certification requires that all U.S. and non-U.S. organizations must certify, before being awarded a grant or cooperative agreement, that the organization does not provide material support or resources for terrorism.

USAID Vetted All Applicable New Prime Awards Made in Fiscal Year 2008

USAID vetted the appropriate officials for all four new prime awards made in fiscal year 2008 that required vetting according to Mission Order 21.[16] In addition, USAID officials said they vetted, in fiscal year 2008, 1,239 individuals in compliance with Mission Order 21 before they received USAID assistance for scholarships, microenterprise loans, and direct cash assistance.

In establishing requirements for whom to vet, a USAID official said the mission has weighed the costs of vetting, the risks of not vetting, and the need to meet its foreign assistance goals. According to this official, the mission does not vet U.S. organizations or citizens who receive assistance due to U.S. privacy law concerns. In addition, U.S. organizations and citizens are subject to U.S. criminal statutes. This USAID official said that they set certain criteria and dollar thresholds that govern whether or not vetting is required. For example, USAID only conducts vetting at the prime and subaward levels and only vets key individuals associated with the applicable non-U.S. organization. As a result, employees of non-U.S. organizations who are not key individuals are not vetted. USAID also does not vet non-U.S. organizations and individuals that receive contracts unless the cumulative value of the contracts received in a 12-month period exceeds $25,000. (See app. II for additional information on the vetting process.)

USAID's New Monthly Subaward Reporting System Did Not Provide Sufficient Information for Us to Assess Compliance

USAID Instituted a New Monthly Subaward Reporting System

USAID instituted a new monthly reporting system in response to a prior GAO recommendation. In 2006, GAO recommended that USAID develop a review and reporting system to help ensure prime awardees comply with the requirements related to subaward vetting, certifications, and mandatory clauses. In response, USAID instituted, as part of its plan to assess compliance, a monthly reporting requirement under which prime awardees (1) submit information on new subawards they have made (including the subawardee name and subaward type and value) and copies of required mandatory clauses and antiterrorism certifications, and (2) indicate whether the required subaward vetting took place prior to the award. The prime awardees are to send the mission a spreadsheet listing the required information for each subaward, as well as copies of the related supporting documentation. The USAID clerk who receives the information inputs the amount of each program-related subaward into the Partner Vetting System (PVS). This allows the mission to track the cumulative amount of contracts awarded to any single awardee to ensure that vetting occurs when required.

Subawards Met Vetting Requirements and Subawardees Provided Required Antiterrorism Certifications

For each of the 51 subawards from our random sample of 95 subawards made to non-U.S. organizations and individuals that required preaward vetting, the PVS showed that USAID vetted and approved each subawardee prior to the date of the subaward.[17] In addition, for each of the 35 subawards below the $25,000 threshold the PVS included the subawardee's name and the amount of the subaward. This information supports the Mission Order 21 requirement to vet a subawardee when the cumulative amount given to that subawardee exceeds $25,000. We also found that prime awardees obtained the signed antiterrorism certification for all six subawards that required this certification.[18] As required, each certification was dated prior to the subaward date.

Insufficient Evidence to Assess Subaward Compliance with Requirements Related to Mandatory Clauses

Based on our random stratified sample, we estimate that 17 percent, plus or minus 7 percentage points, of all fiscal year 2008 subawards identified by USAID did not contain sufficient evidence to determine whether the mandatory clauses were included in the subaward at the time the subaward was made.[19] In conducting our review, we found that the reported information, including the subaward information and related documentation reported monthly to USAID by prime awardees, did not include sufficient evidence to enable us to reasonably conclude whether or not the prime awardee had met the requirement to include the mandatory clauses in the subaward at the time the subaward was made.

The monthly reported information was often insufficient because prime awardees are only required by USAID to provide copies of the mandatory clauses and are not required to include within the mandatory clauses specific references to the subaward, such as the subaward number and date, or to have the subawardee sign and date the clauses. In many instances, the copies of the mandatory clauses provided by prime awardees did not contain information identifying the applicable subaward or otherwise clearly show that the clauses were included in the subawards at the time they were made. Therefore, we asked USAID to provide us with copies of the complete subaward documents for each of our 144 randomly selected subawards. However, even with the copies of actual subaward documents provided by USAID, we could not determine whether the mandatory clauses were included at the time the subaward was made for many of the subawards in our sample.

We based our estimate that approximately 17 percent of all fiscal year 2008 subawards USAID had identified did not contain sufficient evidence to assess compliance on 40 subawards from our random sample. All 40 involved purchase orders issued by 1 prime awardee. For each of the 40 subawards, we found that the information USAID provided was not sufficient to assess compliance because the purchase order documents did not contain the mandatory clauses or include a specific reference to them even though the October 2007 revisions to Mission Order 21 required that the mandatory clauses be included in each contract or grant agreement, including purchase orders. The information provided by USAID consisted of a discrete purchase order and separate additional pages containing the mandatory clauses. However, the only references to the purchase orders that were included on the copies of the mandatory clauses were individual handwritten annotations. It was not clear who made the annotations and when they were made. USAID officials said they believe the subaward information they provided was sufficient to determine compliance because the prime awardee provided USAID with copies of the separate purchase order and mandatory clauses attached together. However, we found several instances in which copies of the same mandatory clauses were provided to us as support for different purchase orders in our subaward sample even though these clauses were signed and dated with dates that were not consistent with the dates of the individual subawards.[20] As a result, we could not reasonably conclude whether or not the prime awardee complied with the requirement to include the mandatory clauses as part of the 40 subawards at the time they were made. To clearly establish at the time of the subaward that subawardees agreed to the mandatory clauses when the mandatory clauses are not included within a subaward , we believe that

- each applicable contract (including purchase orders) or agreement should include a direct and specific reference to the existence and applicability of the separate mandatory clauses, and
- each set of related but separate mandatory clauses should include within the clauses specific and direct reference to the contract (including purchase orders) or agreement.

Some Prime Awardees Did Not Comply with Mandatory Clause Requirements when They Made Subawards

Based on our random stratified sample, we estimate that about 83 percent, plus or minus 7 percentage points, of all fiscal year 2008 USAID-identified subawards contain sufficient evidence to assess compliance.[21] There were 104 subawards in our random sample for which we obtained sufficient documentation to determine whether the prime awardees complied with requirements related to mandatory clauses. We concluded, based on this documentation, that some prime awardees did not always comply with requirements by including mandatory clauses in subaward files at the time they made the subaward. We estimate that for 95 percent, plus or minus 4 percentage points, of those subawards with sufficient information to assess compliance, prime awardees included the mandatory clauses at the time the subaward was made, and, thus were in compliance with Mission Order 21. However, based on the evidence provided to us, we estimate that for 5 percent, plus or minus 4 percentage points, of subawards with sufficient information to assess compliance, the prime awardee did not include the mandatory clauses at the time the subawards were made.

For 14 of the 104 sampled subawards with sufficient information, the evidence provided by USAID established that the prime awardee did not include the required mandatory clauses in each applicable subaward at the time the subaward was made. For 2 of the 14 subawards, the prime awardees later modified the subaward to incorporate the mandatory clauses. For another 8 of the 14 subawards, the prime awardee subsequently obtained the subawardee's acknowledgement that the mandatory clauses were applicable to the subaward by having the subawardee sign and date the mandatory clauses. For 3 other subawards, while the prime awardee made some efforts to incorporate the required mandatory clauses, the required clauses were not included in each applicable subaward prior to the completion of work. For the remaining subaward, the subaward was already completed when the prime awardee noted that the subaward did not include the required mandatory clauses.

State and UNRWA Have Strengthened Policies and Procedures to Determine Whether UNRWA's Actions Are Consistent with Its Agreement to Conform with Conditions for Receiving U.S. Funds, but Weaknesses Remain

UNRWA has agreed with State to take steps to conform with the condition on U.S. contributions set forth in section 30 1(c) of the Foreign Assistance Act of 1961, as amended, and report to State on its efforts semiannually. However, State has not established criteria to determine whether UNRWA is in conformance with conditions on U.S. funds, though it has strengthened some oversight procedures. UNRWA has strengthened policies and procedures intended to conform with the conditions on U.S. contributions, but we found some weaknesses in UNRWA's efforts, such as screening only against a UN terrorist list, in accordance with UN policy, and in internal audits of UNRWA operations.

UNRWA Has Agreed to Conform with Conditions on U.S. Contributions through Agreements with State

Since late 2006, UNRWA and State have signed 3 annual Frameworks for Cooperation and more than 10 letters confirming UNR WA's commitment to conform with the condition on U.S. contributions provided in section 301(c) prior to receiving U.S. funds. In accepting U.S. government funding, UNRWA certifies that it is taking all possible measures to ensure that no part of the United States contribution is being used to furnish assistance to, among others, any refugee who has engaged in any act of terrorism. Under the Framework for Cooperation, which is renewed annually and signed by both State and UNRWA, UNRWA commits to, among other things, (1) conform with the condition in section 301(c) and (2) report every 6 months on actions it has taken to ensure conformance with the condition in section 301(c). UNRWA agrees to similar terms and conditions in U.S. contribution letters before receiving U.S. funds. Since October 2006, UNRWA has submitted five semiannual reports to State, which describe the agency's actions to enforce rules and regulations on staff and beneficiary behavior; monitor UNRWA facilities in the West Bank and Gaza; and screen names of individuals and entities who receive UNRWA funding against a UN terrorist list.

According to UNRWA officials, the policies and procedures UNRWA established to implement the UN principles of neutrality and impartiality and the goals of the International Convention for the Suppression of the Financing of Terrorism support UNRWA's conformance with U.S. conditions. State officials also told us they agreed that UNRWA's efforts to ensure neutrality are consistent with and support UNRWA's efforts to meet the condition for receiving U.S. contributions under section 301(c). Under the UN principles of neutrality and impartiality, UNRWA staff and other personnel should neither seek nor accept instructions from any government or other authority external to UNRWA. This ensures that staff and other personnel are not involved in conduct that is inconsistent with the independence and impartiality required by their status as international civil servants or service providers to the UN. UNRWA officials said UN neutrality is compatible with section 30 1(c) funding conditions. According to UNRWA, a staff member's involvement in a militant group or terrorist activities would be clearly contrary to UNRWA's staff regulations and rules and would certainly result in termination. In requiring that staff, third parties, and facilities be neutral, UNRWA proscribes a range of conduct broader than the conduct described in section 301(c). According to UNRWA rules, staff member involvement in activities such as running for political office in an election or making public political statements would result in disciplinary action, including termination. Although UNRWA does not require beneficiaries to be politically neutral to receive assistance, the agency promotes neutrality within the refugee camps and refuses assistance to refugees involved in inappropriate behavior, including section 301(c)-related activities. UNRWA defines terrorism according to the 1999 International Convention for the Suppression of Financing of Terrorism.[22]

State Has Not Established Criteria to Determine UNRWA's Conformance with Conditions on U.S. Funds but Has Strengthened Some Oversight Procedures

State Has Not Established Criteria to Determine UNRWA's Conformance with Conditions on U.S. Funds

State reported that it has contributed nearly $340 million to UNRWA in the last 2 fiscal years, but State has not established written criteria to determine whether UNRWA's efforts are consistent with the section 301(c) conditions that UNRWA has agreed to for receiving U.S. funds. Aside from the assessments by State whether to continue funding UNRWA,[23] State officials said that they have not developed any written criteria to analyze UNRWA's semiannual reports and have not assessed UNRWA's efforts against such criteria to determine conformance. For example, State has not defined what would constitute nonconformance or developed written definitions of key terms, including "all possible measures"—a concern we also raised in 2003[24]—that would help serve as criteria for analyzing UNRWA's semiannual reports. In addition, we found that State did not have several important UNRWA policy documents, which officials could use to help form criteria for their evaluation of UNRWA's conformance, such as UNRWA instructions for providing relief and social services (including cash assistance) to refugees and the agency's assessment of high-risk areas.

State officials said they consider UNRWA to be in conformance with its commitment to adhere to section 30 1(c) based on State's ongoing review of UNRWA's activities and reports through written communications and discussions with UNRWA officials. State officials told us that, to be consistent with section 30 1(c), they must affirm that State has an internal level of confidence that UNRWA has taken all possible measures to ensure that terrorists are not receiving assistance, such as having procedures in place and taking measures to respond to issues that arise. State officials said that they undertake immediate reviews of any information or allegations of possible concern. State officials told us that their reviews consist of an evaluation of information received from UNRWA and other sources about the allegations or questions arising from a review of the semiannual reports. State officials also note that they regularly follow up, when necessary, on what investigations and disciplinary actions UNRWA undertakes. For example, when an allegation arose that UNRWA had employed a member of Islamic Jihad, State contacted UNRWA to determine how UNRWA handled the allegation. According to State, UNRWA reported that its investigation into the matter resulted in the termination of the employee's direct supervisors.

State Has Strengthened Some Policies and Procedures to Oversee UNRWA's Conformance with U.S. Conditions

Despite the absence of a written evaluation by State of UNRWA's conformance with U.S. conditions, we found that State has strengthened some policies and procedures to oversee UNRWA's conformance with conditions on U.S. funds. In 2003, we reported that State had not defined "terrorism" for the purpose of implementing section 301(c),[25] but State has since concurred with UNRWA in its use of the definition of terrorism contained in the International Convention for the Suppression of the Financing of Terrorism. In addition, State reported that since we began our review it has introduced several new policies and procedures to improve oversight by enhancing communication with UNRWA on section 30 1(c). For example, State officials revised the job description of the Regional Refugee Coordinator responsible for UNRWA to specifically include additional roles and responsibilities for monitoring and reporting on section 301(c) conformance. Also, since we began our review, State has developed additional formal communication procedures to communicate with UNRWA on section 30 1(c) issues. Specifically, State has introduced the following procedures:

- Monthly senior-level conversations between State's Bureau of Population, Refugees and Migration (PRM) and UNRWA on section 301(c) and other priority issues. State told us that senior State officials began meeting with UNRWA in October 2008 to specifically discuss section 301(c)-related issues, including a recent meeting with the Director of UNRWA's Gaza field office.
- Bimonthly meetings between the Regional Refugee Coordinator and the U.S.-funded Operation Support Officers (OSO) for the West Bank

and Gaza who inspect UNRWA facilities, as well as other relevant officials, to discuss section 30 1(c) issues.

- Meetings between PRM Washington, D.C., staff and West Bank and Gaza OSOs to discuss section 301(c) issues during monitoring visits to the region. State officials reported that the Regional Refugee Coordinator and senior State officials from headquarters have met with West Bank and Gaza OSOs six times from November 2008 to April 2009.
- An exchange of letters between State and UNRWA when incidents that are potentially related to section 30 1(c) occur. State recently communicated with UNRWA in a formal letter regarding issues in its most recent semiannual compliance report.

In response to a suggestion we made during our review, State is currently assessing the technical feasibility and resources involved in identifying UNRWA contractors and funding recipients that may be on the U.S. Department of Treasury's Office of Foreign Assets Control (OFAC) list of individuals and entities subject to U.S. sanctions, as well as consulting internally in order to determine whether and how it would undertake such an effort. We discussed with State the feasibility of screening the names of UNRWA contractors and funding recipients against the OFAC list to determine whether UNRWA funds are going to individuals and entities of concern to the United States. As we noted earlier, USAID recommends that all U.S. and non-U.S. organizations that sign the antiterrorism certification consider following steps that include screening names against the OFAC list before providing any material support or resources to an individual or entity. UNRWA declined a past request by State to screen names against the OFAC list on the grounds that doing so contradicts UN policy.[26] When we compared a list of about 15,000 contractors UNRWA paid between 2002 and 2009 to the OFAC list, we found no perfect matches but did find a few possible matches.[27] One of these possible matches was a telecommunications contractor UNRWA paid between 2002 and March 2009, which OFAC placed on its list in July 2008 for reasons related to allegations of corruption. State officials said they would need to discuss with UNRWA what the agency would do with any information regarding such possible matches, given the UN's practice of using a UN terrorist list rather than lists provided by individual UN member governments. UNRWA officials told us that if they are notified of potential matches, they would use the information as a trigger to conduct their own investigation into the matter in accordance with their existing procedures.

According to UNRWA officials, this is in keeping with UNRWA's practice, which is to take seriously and pursue any credible information it receives regarding the possible violation of UN neutrality and impartiality principles.

UNRWA Has Strengthened Policies and Procedures Intended to Conform with U.S. Conditions on Contributions, but Limitations Exist

UNRWA Reported Denying Refugees Benefits, Including Cash Assistance, Due to Inappropriate Conduct

UNRWA reported denying approximately 110 applications for discretionary cash assistance to refugees since July 2006 because agency investigations found the refugees' behavior was inconsistent with UN neutrality or restrictions related to section 301(c).[28] For example, UNRWA reportedly refused burial, rehousing, and other cash assistance to refugees following its investigations into the death of beneficiaries or their spouses as a result of Israeli military incursions and operations, including targeted killings, home demolitions, or workshop damage from shelling by Israeli military authorities. According to UNRWA officials, such incidents are triggers for an UNRWA investigation to determine whether individuals were involved in inappropriate behavior and the potential denial of benefits. In addition, UNRWA reported that it has denied cash assistance for burial expenses to families of beneficiaries it found were killed by an explosion while allegedly preparing an explosive device, as well as refused cash assistance for post-surgery social care to an individual involved in such an explosion. In more than 100 other cases, UNRWA reported that it refused cash assistance to individuals whose homes were demolished or for burial of family members killed in the Israeli operations. The agency reported that it conducted field investigations following these Israeli operations, but could not find clear evidence that the individuals concerned had engaged in an act of terrorism or other inappropriate behavior. However, the agency reported that it denied assistance in these cases based on other reasons it identified in its investigations, including failure to meet some eligibility criteria, competing priorities, or insufficient resources.

UNRWA officials reported that it applies policies and procedures on assistance to refugees that further the agency's conformance with section 30 1(c) conditions. However, they also said that UNRWA provides assistance in the context of its humanitarian mandate, meaning that agency policy is generally not to deny education or primary healthcare benefits. For example, UNRWA officials told us that the child of a refugee who was denied benefits because of section 301(c)-related behavior would not be disqualified from attending an UNRWA school. Similarly, the family of such an individual would remain eligible for medical services at an UNRWA health clinic. In some exceptional cases, officials stated that UNRWA would not provide education benefits to a refugee. For example, UNRWA told us the agency would deny vocational training benefits to a young adult UNRWA found to be involved in inappropriate behavior.

UNRWA Reported Disciplining and Terminating Staff due to Behavior Inconsistent with Agency Policies

UNRWA reported investigating more than 30 cases since October 2006 relating to staff activities that were political or otherwise inconsistent with UN neutrality and taking disciplinary action, including termination, against 7 UNRWA staff as a result of these investigations. UNRWA also reported that four terminated staff members filed appeals with the Joint Appeals Board, of which UNRWA's Commissioner-General dismissed two and two remain ongoing. For example, in the last two years, UNRWA reportedly terminated a staff member's employment immediately upon his release from Israeli detention for conspiring to kidnap an Israeli security officer. UNRWA also reported that it terminated staff members for political activity found to be inconsistent with the independence and impartiality expected of UNRWA staff.[29] UNRWA officials also indicated that they denied benefits to the families of staff members who were found, through investigations, to have been involved in inappropriate behavior. For example, after the agency conducted an investigation into the matter, UNRWA reportedly denied benefits, including pension benefits, to the family of a staff member who was identified by Israeli authorities as a militant and was killed by an Israeli military strike. UNRWA reported that it also terminated two other staff members for management failures in this case.

UNRWA has implemented several policies to promote staff behavior that supports UN neutrality. For example, the UNRWA Organizational Development plan introduced additional training to improve staff knowledge on UN privileges and immunities and legal capacity in all field offices.[30] The agency also reported that it performs reference checks and background security clearances for job applicants and has established procedures to investigate inappropriate staff behavior. UNRWA also told us that it seeks information from authorities whenever staff are detained, convicted, or refused a permit or targeted by Israeli military forces. UNRWA officials said they share the names of all UNRWA staff annually with the governments of Egypt, Israel, Jordan, Lebanon, Syria, and the Palestinian Authority but have received no information on staff members from these governments. Additionally, once hired, UNRWA international staff must apply for visas from the Governments of Egypt, Israel, Jordan, Lebanon, and Syria to work in those areas. UNRWA officials told us that these processes provide regional governments, notably in Egypt, Israel, Jordan, Lebanon, and Syria, with additional opportunities to scrutinize the profiles of UNRWA staff. Additionally, local staff in the West Bank and Gaza must apply for permits from the Government of Israel for transit between certain areas. For additional information on these policies and procedures, see appendix III.

While UNRWA Reported Monitoring Facilities and Finding No Material Misuse, It Continues to Face Recurring Incursions into Facilities

Operation Support Officers (OSO) reported no instances in which agency facilities were not being used as intended, but UNRWA continues to face recurring incursions into its facilities.[31] OSOs are to formally inspect each UNRWA facility in the West Bank and Gaza every 3 to 4 months—and informally inspect the facilities during camp visits as often as possible—to ensure that UNRWA facilities are used only to provide UNRWA aid and services, follow up on the condition of the facilities, and report on and immediately address any issues that are identified. OSOs are also responsible for removing political posters and communicating the importance of UNRWA's neutrality to the community during camp visits. Since July 2006 UNRWA has reported more than 150 incursions into, and other violations of the immunity of, UNRWA facilities by armed Israeli military or police forces, Palestinian security forces, Palestinian militants or individual Palestinians. For example, Israeli forces reportedly used UNRWA school and health facilities as shooting positions or for interrogations, and Palestinian Authority security forces have also reportedly entered UNRWA facilities. In addition, UNRWA reported that armed Palestinian militants have forcibly entered or fired weapons at, near, or from UNRWA schools. Individual Palestinian beneficiaries who were angered by a reduction in UNRWA programming have also taken action against UNRWA facilities. UNRWA regularly protests these types of incursions as violations of its privileges and immunities under international law, and has asked the Palestinian Authority for increased police protection in cases involving Palestinian militants.

UNRWA has introduced formal OSO inspection goals for the Gaza area of three inspections per installation per year, which were absent in prior years, but UNRWA officials reported that the security situation and problems accessing the areas has increased the difficulty of meeting these goals. UNRWA reported that OSOs conducted nearly 1,100 formal inspections of its facilities in the West Bank and Gaza in 2008, meeting approximately 95 percent of its goal. In the West Bank, OSOs formally inspected each facility approximately 3.6 times (916 total inspections) in 2008, narrowly missing a goal of 4 inspections per installation (1024 total inspections). In Gaza, OSOs conducted 172 formal inspections in 2008.

However, this represents less than one inspection per installation in the Gaza area.

UNRWA currently does not have an OSO program in Jordan, Lebanon, or Syria, but according to UNRWA officials, the agency hopes to receive funding that will enable it to expand the OSO program to Lebanon. In May, UNRWA selected a new protection officer funded by the European Commission to integrate the refugees' protection into UNRWA operations in Lebanon, including monitoring and reporting to senior staff on protection-related issues. State has reported that it approved funding in April 2009 for an expansion of the OSO program to Lebanon. We found that facility inspections under the OSO program may address conditions that could undermine UNRWA's neutrality. For example, during our visit to an UNRWA school in Jordan, where UNRWA does not currently operate an OSO program, we saw political graffiti on an exterior wall and posters created by teachers to support the school's human rights curriculum that had some violent content. Since our visit, UNRWA officials reported that the Jordan field office has called upon senior field officials to inspect facilities and that West Bank OSOs have shared practices with these officials to improve their ability to perform functions similar to the OSOs.

UNRWA Reported Expanding Screening with a UN Security Council List and Finding No Matches, but the Screening Process Has Limitations

UNRWA told us that it has expanded its use of a UN Security Council terrorist list to now screen all recipients of agency funds and that none of its staff, contractors, beneficiaries, or microfinance clients have appeared on the list, but we found some limitations in the agency's screening process. UNRWA screens its staff and contractors every 6 months against the UN 1267 list. In addition, for the first time, UNRWA screened all 4.6 million Palestinian refugees and microfinance clients against this list in December 2008. UNRWA officials told us that in addition to its screening and investigations of individual applicants prior to providing assistance, the agency intends to make such UN 1267 screening of all registered refugees and microfinance clients a routine procedure. The agency also enhanced transparency by introducing, in February 2009, a policy to disclose on its Web site details of UNRWA contracts valued over $100,000, which includes contractor names it screens against the UN 1267 list. However, the list is limited to those individuals or entities affiliated with Al-Qaida and the Taliban and thus does not specifically include major regional groups, such as Hamas and Hezbollah, which the United States has designated as foreign terrorist organizations.32 According to UNRWA, the UN Security Council has various working groups for terrorism-related issues, but the Sanctions Committee's UN 1267 list is currently the only such UN terrorist screening list available.33 In addition, UNRWA does not conduct pre-employment screening of staff. UNRWA stated that screening every 6 months ensures that staff are screened during employment probationary periods. Furthermore, UNRWA told us it is unable to screen all persons displaced by the 1967 conflict who are receiving health and education benefits because the agency does not register or collect information on such displaced persons in the region.

Internal Audits of UNRWA Do Not Assess Antiterrorism Controls or the Overall Cash Assistance Program

UNRWA internal audits of its operations do not explicitly assess antiterrorism controls or controls for UNRWA's overall cash assistance program. UNRWA reported recent efforts to expand the capacity of its Department of Internal Oversight Services, which evaluates the agency's financial accounts, assesses the risk of fraud, and reviews the adequacy and effectiveness of internal controls systems, by hiring additional audit staff.[34] However, UNRWA officials reported that the department has not audited signed agency contracts to determine if staff physically attach the General Conditions of Contract, which include an antiterrorism clause and which must be in every contract between UNRWA and a contractor. UNRWA told us that the legal department ensures that all contracts contain these clauses. The Department of Internal Oversight Services also reported on an agency-wide risk management effort to identify high-risk areas in 2008 and has planned audits related to UNRWA's internal justice system and emergency assistance activities in the West Bank and Gaza funded by the agency's Emergency Appeal request to donors. However, audits related to several high-risk areas identified in the risk management exercise, such as the Special Hardship

Assistance Program in Gaza and Syria,[35] camp reconstruction activities in Lebanon and oversight in Gaza are contingent on the availability of resources. In addition, since 2007, this department has conducted five reviews related to UNRWA staff screening processes and fraud prevention and detection, but none focused on UNRWA's cash assistance program activities funded through the General Fund or Emergency Appeal, such as cash subsidies for food or selective or emergency cash assistance. UNRWA reported, however, that approximately 10 percent of the department's work involves a review of a food aid and cash assistance program. The European Commission funds both the assistance program and its review. UNRWA told us that future internal audits would assess UNRWA's compliance with its neutrality and antiterrorism policies for contractors, as well as internal controls for cash assistance. According to agency officials, this will have resource implications for the agency.

While internal audits have not focused on UNRWA's overall cash assistance activities, the UN Board of Auditors, UNRWA's external auditor, reported on instances of breakdowns or weaknesses in internal controls.[36] UNRWA officials reported that after the agency investigated a case of cash assistance fraud in Gaza, the agency conducted a thorough reform of cash management procedures and held the senior managers of the program accountable for the systemic weaknesses identified and, in doing so, requested and accepted the early retirement of the 2 most senior program staff. Specifically, UNRWA reported that following this incident, the Gaza field office suspended emergency cash assistance (other than for shelter) to individuals and focused cash assistance instead on clearly defined target groups such as students enrolled in UNRWA schools and refugees enrolled in the Special Hardship program. In addition, UNRWA told us that it integrated its Emergency Cash Assistance program into a stand-alone Emergency Program, which includes a unit to monitor the integrity of emergency services.

CONCLUSIONS

It is an important U.S. goal to have processes in place to help ensure that U.S. funding for Palestinian assistance programs is not provided to individuals or entities engaged in terrorist activities. In recent years, USAID, State, and UNRWA have strengthened their policies and procedures to help ensure that assistance is not inadvertently provided to terrorists. In response to our 2006 recommendation, USAID has clarified its guidance and improved its system for vetting certain recipients of USAID assistance, thereby significantly decreasing its vetting times. In addition, State and UNRWA have agreed on a definition of terrorism, which addresses a concern we raised in 2003.

USAID complied with all applicable antiterrorism-related requirements when making its new prime awards in fiscal year 2008. Regarding prime awardees' fiscal year 2008 subawards identified by USAID, required vetting occurred and applicable antiterrorism certifications were obtained. However, we estimate that for approximately 17 percent of the fiscal year 2008 subawards identified by USAID, there was not sufficient information to assess compliance. For the remaining subawards, we estimate that 5 percent did not contain the mandatory clauses at the time the subaward was made. In addition, the subaward information reported by prime awardees was not always sufficient to monitor compliance. Action needs to be taken to help ensure that mandatory clauses are included within each document and that prime awardees provide USAID with sufficient monthly information to clearly demonstrate that mandatory clauses have been included in applicable subawards.

State has strengthened policies and procedures to determine whether UNRWA's efforts are consistent with its agreement to conform to U.S. conditions on funds by, for example, recently introducing additional mechanisms for communicating on section 30 1(c) issues with UNRWA. However, State has neither defined criteria for evaluating UNRWA's conformance with its commitment for accepting U.S. funds nor screened names of UNRWA contractors against the OFAC list. UNRWA has strengthened its policies and procedures to conform with conditions on U.S. funds, such as expanding screening of all recipients of UNRWA funds against the UN 1267 list, but UNRWA's internal audits do not determine whether UNRWA contractors have signed contracts that include the required antiterrorism clause or assess controls for UNRWA's overall cash assistance program. Addressing these weaknesses would provide greater assurance that assistance is not inadvertently being provided to terrorists.

Recommendations for Executive Action

To strengthen compliance with USAID policies and procedures at the subaward level, we recommend that the Administrator of USAID take action to help ensure that

- the mandatory clauses are included within each subaward contract or agreement or, when not included within the contract or agreement there is sufficient evidence to clearly establish that the subawardee has agreed to comply with mandatory clauses at the time the award is made; and
- prime awardees provide sufficiently detailed information in their monthly subaward reports to clearly demonstrate that mandatory clauses were included in the subaward at the time the award was made.

To help ensure that assistance is not inadvertently provided to terrorists, we recommend that the Secretary of State consider taking additional steps to oversee UNRWA's conformance with U.S. conditions on funding, such as (1) establishing criteria to evaluate UNRWA's efforts; (2) screening the names of UNRWA contractors against lists of individuals and entities of concern to the United States; and (3) monitoring UNRWA's commitment that future internal audits would assess UNRWA's compliance with its neutrality and antiterrorism policies for contractors as well as internal controls for cash assistance.

AGENCY COMMENTS AND OUR EVALUATION

USAID, State, and UNRWA provided written comments on a draft of this report (see app. IV, V, and VI). USAID, State, and UNRWA outlined actions they plan to take to implement our recommendations. USAID stated that our work contributed positively to the continuous improvement and strengthening of USAID West Bank and Gaza mission's compliance with antiterrorism policies and procedures. However, USAID disagreed with the extent of our finding that insufficient evidence was present to assess whether a significant percentage of subawards were in compliance. We maintain that evidence was insufficient because the only references to the purchase orders that were included on the mandatory clauses were individual handwritten annotations. It was not clear who made the annotations and when those annotations were made. To implement our recommendations USAID stated that it will issue new instructions to the mission's prime awardees to help ensure that contracts and agreements contain clear and specific references to attached clauses and clauses likewise contain clear and specific references to the base agreement. USAID also plans to instruct prime awardees to explain any inconsistencies in their monthly subaward reports. Additionally, USAID will require prime awardees to certify that their monthly subaward reports are both accurate and complete.

State recognized that it is appropriate for the department to consider taking additional steps to further ensure that U.S. assistance to UNRWA is not inadvertently provided to terrorists. State concurred with two parts of our recommendation. State said that it will work with UNRWA to develop criteria, as appropriate, as well as reporting requirements, which will be documented in State and UNRWA's Framework for Cooperation for 2010. State also said that the internal audits we recommended would prove beneficial to UNRWA's operations and conformance with section 30 1(c) and noted UNRWA's written commitment to conduct internal audits of key UNRWA processes. State is actively assessing the feasibility of screening names of UNRWA contractors against lists of individuals and entities of concern to the United States. State said that addressing two parts of our recommendation will have resource implications for State and UNRWA, since additional resources would be required to effectively screen names and conduct additional internal UNRWA audits.

UNRWA also welcomed our report and findings and made a commitment that future internal UNRWA audits would assess the agency's compliance with its neutrality and antiterrorism policies for contractors and internal controls for cash assistance. UNRWA said it would facilitate State's monitoring of this commitment and work with State to develop criteria for UNRWA's conformance to section 301(c). In addition, USAID, State and UNRWA provided technical comments on a draft of this report, which we have incorporated as appropriate.

We are sending copies of this report to other congressional offices, State, USAID, and UNRWA. The report also is available at no charge on the GAO Web site at http://www.gao.gov.

If you or your staff have any questions about this report, please contact me at (202) 512-9601 or melitot@gao.gov. Contact points for our Offices of Congressional Relations and Public Affairs may be found on the last page of this report. Other contacts and major contributors are listed in appendix VII.

Thomas Melito
Director,
International Affairs and Trade

List of Congressional Committees

The Honorable Howard L. Berman Chairman
The Honorable Ileana Ros-Lehtinen Ranking Member
Committee on Foreign Affairs
House of Representatives

The Honorable Gary L. Ackerman Chairman
The Honorable Dan Burton
Ranking Member
Subcommittee on the Middle East and South Asia
Committee on Foreign Affairs House of Representatives

The Honorable Patrick Leahy
Chairman
The Honorable Judd Gregg
Ranking Member
Subcommittee on State, Foreign
Operations, and Related Programs Committee on Appropriations
United States Senate

The Honorable Nita M. Lowey Chair
The Honorable Kay Granger Ranking Member
Subcommittee on State, Foreign Operations,
and Related Programs
Committee on Appropriations House of Representatives

APPENDIX I: OBJECTIVES, SCOPE, AND METHODOLOGY

Our objectives were to (1) assess the extent to which the U.S. Agency for International Development (USAID) has complied with its policies and procedures to help ensure that its p rograms do not provide support to entities or individuals associated with terrorism in the West Bank and Gaza and (2) assess the Department of State's (State) and UNRWA's policies and proce dures to support conformance with U.S. statutory conditions placed on contributions provided to UNRWA to prohibit funding of terrorist-related activities.

USAID Policies and Procedures

To determine the extent to which the USAID Mission to the West Bank and Gaza (the mission) complied--at the prime and subaward levels--with its policies and procedures to help ensure that its programs do not provide support to entities or individuals associated with terrorism in the West Bank and Gaza, we identified relevant legal and other requirements as well as USAID policies and procedures to comply with those requirements. These legal and other requirements are contained in U.S. appropriations laws, executive orders, and the U.S. code. Mission Order 21 is the mission's primary document that details the procedures to comply with applicable laws and executive orders to help ensure that assistance does not provide support to entities or individuals associated with terrorism. The mission revised Mission Order 21 effective October 3, 2007 to update its antiterrorism procedures in response to, among other things, recommendations we made in a 20 06 report.

We discussed the mission's imp lementation of Mission Order 21 with the USAID Mission Director, senior staff, regional legal advisor, program staff, and other officials responsible for managing assistance projects and overseeing contracts, grants, and cooperative agreements at the USAID Missio n in Tel Aviv, Israel, and the U.S. Consulate in Jerusalem. We also interviewed five of USAID's implementing partners that had received relatively large do llar contracts from USAID in the West Bank, Jerusalem, and the United States. We interviewed State, USAID, and other officials involved in vetting USAID award recipients. In addition, we interviewed USAID's Regional Inspector General in Cairo to determine the results of audits of West Bank and Gaza assistance programs and steps taken to strengthen USAID's auditing procedures.

We focused our review on the mission's prime award contracts, grants, and cooperative agreements and subawards that were made during fiscal year 2008 through the Economic Support Fund, in accordance with the mandate contained in the Consolidated Appropriations Act for fiscal year 2008 (PL 110-161). To determine whether the mission's prime awards contained the applicable antiterrorism certification and clauses as required by Mission Order 21, we reviewed copies of all 32 new prime awards issued by the mission during fiscal year 2008. To determine whether the subawards complied with relevant Mission Order 21 requirements, we selected a random stratified sample of 95 subawards made to non-U.S. organizations and 49 subawards made to U.S. organizations, a total of 144 subawards. Initially, we selected a random sample of 147 subawards. However, because one of the reported subawards (to a U.S. organization) identified by USAID was not actually executed, we had a random sample of 146 subawards. We also removed from the sample 2 subawards that did not require mandatory clauses, resulting in a random stratified sample of 144 subawards. Our sample of 49 subawards made to U.S. organizations was drawn from a subpopulation of 101 subawards and our sample of 95 subawards made to non-U.S. organizations was drawn from a subpopulation of 2,519 subawards. We selected these subaward sample sizes to estimate compliance rates with confidence intervals of no more than plus or minus 10 percent for both the U.S. organizations and the non-U.S. organizations. The percentages we report for all subawards are weighted to reflect the fact that we oversampled the U.S. subawards in order to ensure that we obtained a sufficient number for making projections for that strata.

We selected these random stratified samples from a universe of 2 ,620 new fiscal year 2008 subawards identified by the mission based on subaward activity reported to the mission by prime awardees. The mission developed the universe by assembling the subaward spreadsheets that were available as of October 2008 and provided by each partner who had an active prime award during the period from October 3, 2007 through September 30, 2008. The spreadsheets included U.S. and non-U.S. subawards. From the subawards reported on these spreadsheets, the mission identified subawards made during the period from October 1, 2007 through September 30, 2008 and filtered out all subawards made outside of those dates. The mission then created a list containing the names of the organizations receiving each subaward and the start and end date of each subaward. At our request, the mission then added information to the list to include the amount and type of each subaward (e.g. contract, grant). In addition, if the mission found a subaward reported in New Israeli Shekels, it replaced the amount in shekels with an estimated conversion to U.S. dollars to help facilitate the GAO selection process. In addition, if the mission found an entry with an end date listed as "immediately," it replaced this word with a date identical to the start date. The mission's objective was to include all individual subaward agreements and exclude any extensions and modifications to those awards. However, accordin g to the mission, their attempt to exclude extensions and modifications was limited to those instances in which the information was available from the prime awardee's monthly reports. As a result, our sample included several modifications and extensions. In addition, our sample included 2 instances in which prime awardees bundled multiple procurements and reported them as a single subaward. We did not attempt to corre ct for these cases, but instead made a modification to the decision rules we used to determine compliance.

We examined in detail (1) the vetting documentation maintained by the mission on its Partner Vetting System (PVS) to determine if the mission had vetted non-U.S. prime awardees and a sample of subawardees as required by Mission Order 21 and (2) prime award and subaward documentation for a sample of subawardees to determine if the antiterrorism certifications were signed and the mandatory clauses were included in the prime awards and subawards as required by Mission Order 21. We reviewed the vetting information in the PVS for all four prime awards made to non-U.S. organizations and a random stratified sample of 95 subawards made to non-U.S. organizations. The remaining 28 prime awards and 49 subawards were made to U.S. organizations, and so were not subject to vetting. We compared the vetting date to the award date to determine if the mission vetted the appropriate non-U.S. organizations prior to the date of award. To understand the mission's vetting process, we interviewed various mission officials including the head of the Program Support Unit, which is the division responsible for the vetting pro cess. To determine whether the subawards contained the required mandatory clauses and whether required antiterrorism certifications were obtained, we reviewed applicable documentation for a random sample of 95 subawards made to non-U.S. organizations and 49 subawards made to U.S. organizations, a total of 144 subawards.

UNRWA Policies and Procedures

To assess UNRWA's and State's policies and procedures to support conformance with U.S. statutory conditions placed on assistance to UNRWA, we reviewed the applicable federal law—section 30 1(c) of the Foreign Assistance Act of 1961, as amended. We also reviewed documentation on 3 Frameworks for Cooperation between State and UNRWA and 10 U.S. contributions letters that describe UNRWA's agreement to conform with U.S. conditions on funds for 2007 through 2009; State's processes for overseeing UNRWA's conformance to U. S. conditions; and documents describing State discussions on UNRWA's conformance to U.S. conditions. We also interviewed State officials in Amman, Jordan; Jerusalem; and Washington D.C., including the Regional Refugee Coordinator in Jerusalem, who are responsible for implementing section 301(c) and overseeing U.S. contributions to UNRWA.

To describe UNRWA policies and procedures to help ensure that all possible measures were taken to assure U.S. funds were not used to furnish assistance to any refugee who, among other things, engaged in any act of terrorism, we reviewed our 2003 report on UNRWA,[1] as well as UNRWA and UN budget, policy, and program documents for fiscal years 2007 and 2008. We also examined five UNRWA semiannual reports on UNRWA's efforts to conform to agreements with U.S. conditions on funds from July 2006 through December 2008. These reports provide data on staff disciplinary actions, denial of benefits to refugees, inspection s of and incursions into UNRWA facilities, and screening of recipients of UNRWA funds against the UN Security Council's Al-Qaida and Taliban Sanctions Committee Consolidated List (UN 1267 list). We also interviewed UNRWA headquarters and field officials in Amman, Jordan and Jerusalem responsible for implementing and overseeing UNRWA's programs, including the Commissioner-General; Deputy Commissioner-General; Directors of UNRWA Field Offices; senior officials in the Departments of Administrative Support, Finance, Internal Oversight, Legal Affairs, and several program offices; and staff responsible for monitoring facilities in the West Bank and Gaza areas. Furthermore, to obtain information on UNRWA's programs and oversight activities in the agency's refugee camp s, we visited three camps in the West Bank and outside Amman (Jalazone, Jabal el-Hussein, and Baqa'a refugee camps) where we spoke with UNRWA staff and Palestinian refugees about their understanding of the agency's policies and procedures. We also met with an official from the government of Israel's Ministry of Foreign Affairs Department for UN Political Affairs.

Additionally, we compared a list of contractors used by UNRWA from 2002 to 2009 with the U.S. Department of Treasury's Office of Foreign Assets Controls (OFAC) Specially Designated Nationals and Blocked Person s list, as of February 3, 2009. Our relatively basic computerized matching comparison focused strictly on the "name" field supplied by UN RWA and OFAC, including both individuals and entities, although information for the place of birth and date of birth fields were available for some individuals in the OFAC list. The UNRWA list contained approximately 20,000 records with names, while the OFAC list contained approximately 9,000 primary names and more than 5,000 aliases. We removed "tokens" or parts of names, such as prefixes or suffixes on names, in each list to make the matching process possible. For the UNRWA list of names, we then removed any name which only comprised one token, such as the name "Ali." The original OFAC list contained a string of information includin g names, dates of birth, and places of birth that were wrapped on multiple lines. After converting the data into a more usable form, taking into account both primary names and aliases, we were able to produce a usable file from the OFAC list with approximately 14,600 names.

Matching was complicated by a number of factors, such as name formats that varied, many names that had been translated from foreign languages , and multiple aliases for some of the individuals named. We addressed these issues to the extent possible with the available software and performed a comparison of these names to produce potential matches between the two lists. While a perfect match between the two lists would require the records in each list to be identically matched, we found that names in the two lists may have varied in terms of the number of tokens , punctuation considerations, the translation of foreign sounding names an d variations in spelling. Therefore, we identified records that were reasonably similar to be potential matches. For each potential match, we performed a manual review of the available information on the records using other Internet sources, to help determine whether these were possible matches. It is worth noting that more sophisticated software, specifically dedicated to the Arabic language that takes into account linguistics or phonetic sounds for each name, may reveal additional information about potential matches.

We conducted this performance audit from August 2008 to May 2009 in accordance with generally accepted government auditing standards. Tho se standards require that we plan and perform the audit to obtain sufficient, appropriate evidence to provide a reasonable basis for our findings and conclusions based on our audit objectives. We believe that the evidence obtained provides a reasonable basis for our findings and conclusions based on our audit objectives.

APPENDIX II: USAID MISSION TO THE WEST BANK AND GAZA VETTING PROCESS

Mission Order 21 states that the USAID Mission to the West Bank and Gaza must vet certain non-U.S. recipients of USAID funding, which involves checking recipients' names and other identifying information against databases and other information sources to determine if they are involved with terrorism. The Program Support Unit (PSU) at the USAID Mission coordinates the vetting process for those requiring vetting, as shown in figure 1.

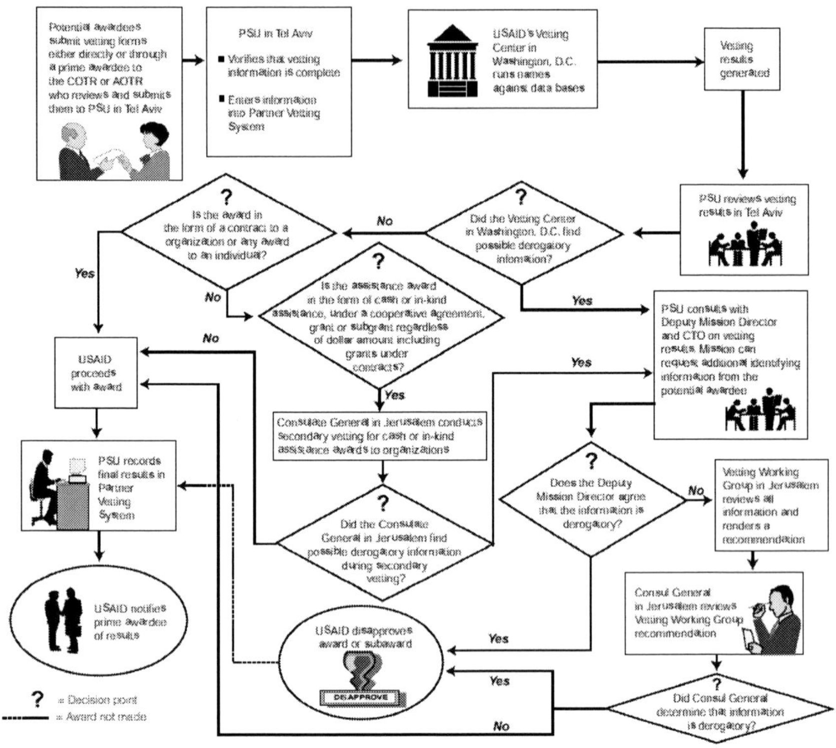

Source: GAO analysis of USAID documents and Art Explosion.

Note: The following acronyms refer to USAID personnel who manage awards: Contracting Officer's Technical Representative (COTR), Agreement Officer's Technical Representative (AOTR), and Cognizant Technical Officer (CTO).

Figure 1. USAID's Vetting Process for Awards to Aid Palestinians, Fiscal Year 2008.

APPENDIX III: UNRWA POLICIES AND PROCEDURES FOR CASH ASSISTANCE, STAFF NEUTRALITY, USE OF UNRWA FACILITIES, AND CONTRACTOR BEHAVIOR

UNRWA has several policies and procedures to help support UN neutrality and UNRWA's conformance with conditions on receiving U.S. funds. This appendix provides additional information on specific policies and procedures that UNRWA uses to implement its cash assistance activities and promote the neutrality of agency staff, facilities, and contractors.

Policies for Cash Assistance to Refugees

Policies for Special Hardship and Cash Assistance

UNRWA has policies to oversee the relief and social services assistance it provides to refugees, including special instructions for Special Hardship, selective, and emergency cash assistance.[1] UNRWA policy is to provide Special Hardship cash subsidies for food only to registered Palestinian refugees. In addition, UNRWA staff are to screen applicants' eligibility for cash assistance. The screening process includes a home visit by a social worker and follow-up checks to ensure assistance has been used for the designated purpose. Under written UNRWA instructions for assistance, if a family has other sources of income, such as Palestinian Authority ministries or charitable organizations, it may be disqualified from receiving UNRWA cash assistance. Agency officials also reported that UNRWA uses a computerized distribution list for Special Hardship cash subsidies for food, which has been reviewed by finance and social services staff in the field. Similarly, agency policy states that senior field staff are responsible for overseeing cash distributions, a social worker is required to be present at each distribution point, and refugees must provide certain documentation to receive cash assistance. In addition, senior officials in the Department of Relief and Social Services are required to conduct random visits and review case files to ensure proper handling of Special Hardship cases by social workers and staff. Social workers are also to rotate among areas to alleviate social pressures they may face from refugees. UNRWA also recently introduced the use of a needs-based formula, the proxy means test formula, as criteria for receipt of certain social services, such as Special Hardship assistance, in order to target benefits to those in most need.

Other Policies for Cash Assistance

UNRWA has additional measures to oversee its cash assistance activities. For example, for both selective and emergency UNRWA cash assistance, UNRWA policy is that social workers are to make field inquiries to examine an applicant's emergency circumstances prior to making a recommendation for assistance. Depending on the amount of assistance recommended, senior relief and social services officials at varying levels of hierarchy must then review the recommendation. Social workers are to conduct follow-up visits with beneficiaries, and senior field officials are to perform random checks to determine whether funds are spent for approved uses. In addition, relief and social services officials in the field must report monthly to the head of the department on any selective or emergency cash assistance approved and issued.

Policies and Procedures to Promote UNRWA Staff Neutrality

UNRWA reported that it has implemented various policies and procedure s to promote staff neutrality, including both pre- and post-hire policies on staff behavior. In cases where UNRWA investigates and finds staff behavior inconsistent with UNRWA policies, UNRWA policy is to discipline or terminate the staff.

General Policies for UNRWA Staff Neutrality

UNRWA reported that it has implemented various policies and procedures to promote staff neutrality. For example, UNRWA requires staff to sign a neutrality pledge in each employment contract and an annual verification statement on outside activities. Officials reported that staff receive information on neutrality policies during their induction upon employment, including training on UNRWA privileges, immunities and responsibilities, and staff receive ongoing guidance from senior officials in the field and headquarters. UNRWA staff rules also require staff members to avoid actions and public pronouncements that may adversely reflect on the integrity, independence and impartiality required by their positions. While UNRWA does not expect staff to give up their national sentiments or their political and religious convictions, the agency requires staff to bear in mind the reserve and tact incumbent upon them by their employment at UNRWA. For instance, staff may exercise their right to vote, but may not engage in any political activity inconsistent with independence and impartiality. UNRWA staff rules and regulations do not prohibit membership in and payment of normal financial contributions to a political party, provided that membership does not obligate, entail or result in statements or actions that violate the staff member's UN neutrality and impartiality obligations.

Prehire Policies for UNRWA Staff Neutrality

Officials reported that UNRWA performs reference checks and background security clearances in accordance with the policies for each field office area and asks whether applicants have been convicted of any crimes prior to hiring them. The screening processes differ by level of st aff responsibility and the type of governance and security structures in the field area. UNRWA conducts background and security screenings with the assistance of the governments of Jordan and Syria in those field areas, under agreements UNRWA negotiated with host governments during early years of agency operations in the 1950s. For example, in Jordan, once a hiring review board has selected a candidate for a position, UNRWA will send the Government of Jordan a formal notice asking if the government has any concerns regarding the individual; the government then performs a security screening. Representatives from the governments of Jordan and Syria are also members of the UNRWA hiring panel in those field areas and may provide input on potential staff. UNRWA reported instances in which a government did not approve of UNRWA hiring an individual, and although UNRWA was not told the reason for the concerns, the individual was not hired. UNRWA also share s the names of all staff with host governments, including Israel and the Palestinian Authority, on an annual basis under the 1946 Convention on the Privileges and Immunities of the United Nations.

Policies for Investigating UNRWA Staff Behavior

UNRWA has also established procedures to investigate inappropriate staff behavior, which may result in the disciplining or termination of staff. For example, investigations may consist of fact-finding investigations or formal Boards of Inquiry involving legal officers or senior management, with the technical assistance of UNRWA's Department of Legal Affairs or Department of Internal Oversight Services. Staff members have an obligation to report misconduct and are protected from retaliation under UNRWA's whistleblower and antireprisal policy, and according to officials, the agency takes swift disciplinary action whenever there is evidence of staff member involvement in inappropriate political or military activities. Officials stated that this disciplinary action is well-known, predictable and consistent, and has a deterrent effect. UNRWA told us the agency also has formal procedures for staff to appeal investigation results through the UNRWA Joint Appeals Board, but the Commissioner General is responsible for all final determinations. Staff may also seek recourse after the UNRWA Joint Appeals Board process through the UN Administrative Tribunal, the decision of which is binding on UNRWA as a UN agency.[2]

Rules and Regulations for the Use of UNRWA Facilities by Outside Entities

UNRWA field offices have established rules and regulations for the use of UNRWA facilities in Jordan, Lebanon, and the West Bank by outside entities, and the Gaza and Syria field offices have a policy of not permitting use of UNRWA facilities by any outside entity. Use of UNRWA facilities in Jordan, Lebanon and the West Bank requires a formal written request and approval by the field office director. Officials reported that a general condition of any UNRWA approval is that the organization using an UNRWA facility respects UN neutrality, and UNRWA may monitor the event. The agency also has a policy of approving use of facilities for nonpolitical activities only. However, UNRWA told us that it does allow governmental authorities to request the use of facilities for polling stations, providing that campaigning is not present. For example, the government of Jordan has used UNRWA schools as polling stations. Officials reported that the agency has also allowed the use of its facilities for other approved purposes, including use by UNRWA summer camps and by international organizations such as the United Nations Children's Fund and World Health Organization. In addition, certain community- based organizations, affiliated to varying extents with UNRWA, may use premises provided by UNRWA in all five fields of operation, pursu ant to conditions in a memorandum of understanding. Officials reported that relief and social services staff work closely with and monitor such organizations.

Policies and Procedures Regarding Contractor Behavior

UNRWA's procurement policies and procedures communicate the agency's expectations for contractor behavior. In addition to its General Conditions for Contract, which includes an antiterrorism clause, when signing contracts with the agency, contractors must also abide by the UN Supplier Code of Conduct, which includes a conflict of interest and corruption clause and outlines corporate policies and practices expected of all UN suppliers. According to UNRWA officials, as a UN agency, UNRWA also checks contractors against the UN Suspended/Removed Vendor Report, which identifies those vendors confirmed to be doing business in an unethical or corrupt manner. Individual contracts are managed by procurement staff in the

Department of Administrative Services, and officials reported that any inappropriate conduct would result in a termination of contract.

APPENDIX IV: COMMENTS FROM THE U.S. AGENCY FOR INTERNATIONAL DEVELOPMENT

Note: A GAO comment supplementing those in the report text appear at the end of this appendix.

USAID
FROM THE AMERICAN PEOPLE

MAY 8 2009

Mr. Thomas Melito, Director
International Affairs and Trade
U.S. Government Accountability Office
441 G Street, N.W.
Washington, D.C. 20548

Dear Mr. Melito:

I am pleased to provide the U.S. Agency for International Development's (USAID) formal response on the draft GAO report entitled "*FOREIGN ASSISTANCE: Measures to Prevent Inadvertent Payments to Terrorists under Palestinian Aid Programs Have Been Strengthened, but Some Weaknesses Remain*" (GAO-09-622). Our comments are limited to those sections of the report concerning USAID's assistance and operations.

The GAO team's field work and draft report contributes positively to the continuous improvement and strengthening of USAID West Bank/Gaza's compliance with antiterrorism policies and procedures. We are pleased to note that the draft GAO report recognized USAID's full compliance with vetting and anti-terrorism certification policies and procedures with respect to both prime awards and the audited subaward sample.

See comment 1.

The GAO's principal finding related to compliance with the inclusion of mandatory clauses in subawards. This finding was based on an estimate that a significant percentage of all fiscal year 2008 subawards do not contain sufficient evidence to assess whether required clauses form part of the subawards. USAID asserts that there is adequate evidence that the mandatory clauses do form part of the awards. USAID contracting officers and other employees familiar with procedures for issuing contracts and grants were able to confirm that the mandatory provisions formed part of each award, with only one exception. As a result, we believe the GAO's assertion of insufficient evidence should be reconsidered.

In either case, there are steps that USAID can take to further strengthen prime awardee file documentation and reporting that will also address the GAO's concerns. In the draft report, the GAO recommends that the Administrator of USAID strengthen compliance with USAID policies and procedures at the

U.S. Agency for International Development
1300 Pennsylvania Avenue, NW
Washington, DC 20523
www.usaid.gov

subaward level by ensuring that: (a) mandatory clauses are included within each subaward contract or agreement, or, when handled outside the contract or agreement there is sufficient evidence to clearly establish that the subawardee has agreed to comply with mandatory clauses at the time the award is made; and (b) prime awardees provide sufficiently detailed information in their monthly subaward reports to clearly demonstrate that mandatory clauses were included in the subaward at the time the award was made.

In order to implement the GAO's recommendations, USAID will issue new instructions to its prime awardees under the West Bank and Gaza program to ensure that contracts and agreements contain clear and specific references to attached clauses and that attached clauses, likewise, contain clear and specific references to the base agreement. Furthermore, prime awardees will also be instructed to explain any inconsistencies between the dates on which mandatory clauses were incorporated into subawards and the dates of the subawards themselves. Lastly, prime awardees will certify to the completeness and accuracy of the monthly subaward report. USAID believes that these new measures, combined with USAID's semi-annual compliance reviews of all prime awardee subaward files, addresses the draft report's underlying concern, namely, ensuring that required clauses are included in subawards at the time the subawards are made. In addition, USAID's proposed action will provide greater assurance that the GAO will have the evidence it requires to audit prime awardee compliance in the future.

Thank you for the opportunity to respond to the GAO draft report and for the courtesies extended by your staff in the conduct of this review.

Sincerely,

Drew W. Luten
Acting Assistant Administrator
Bureau for Management

The following is GAO's comment on USAID's letter dated May 8, 2009.

GAO Comment

1. We maintain that evidence was insufficient to assess compliance because the only references to the purchase orders that were included on the mandatory clauses were individual handwritten annotations. It was not clear who made the annotations and when those annotations were made.

APPENDIX V: COMMENTS FROM THE U.S. DEPARTMENT OF STATE

United States Department of State

Washington, D.C. 20520

MAY 06 2009

Ms. Jacquelyn Williams-Bridgers
Managing Director
International Affairs and Trade
Government Accountability Office
441 G Street, N.W.
Washington, D.C. 20548-0001

Dear Ms. Williams-Bridgers:

We appreciate the opportunity to review your draft report, "FOREIGN ASSISTANCE: Measures to Prevent Inadvertent Payments to Terrorists under Palestinian Aid Programs Have Been Strengthened, but Some Weaknesses Remain," GAO Job Code 320618.

The enclosed Department of State comments are provided for incorporation with this letter as an appendix to the final report.

If you have any questions concerning this response, please contact Monique Ramgoolie, Program Officer, Bureau of Population, Refugees and Migration at (202) 663-3103.

Sincerely,

James L. Millette

cc: GAO – Cheryl Goodman
PRM – Samuel Witten (Acting)
State/OIG – Mark Duda

2

its actions to address any allegations or incidents. We also review closely UNRWA's 301(c) reports, provided to the Department on a semi-annual basis, asking UNRWA for additional details and clarification whenever necessary.

As noted in the GAO report, continued USG funding for UNRWA is contingent upon the Department's conclusion that UNRWA continues to take the steps necessary to meet the condition required by section 301(c). This condition is included in the annual USG-UNRWA Framework for Cooperation as well as in all contribution letters that obligate Migration and Refugee Assistance (MRA) and Emergency Refugee Migration Assistance (ERMA) funds to UNRWA. The Department and UNRWA have worked continuously to enhance both UNRWA's policies and procedures and State/PRM's oversight of UNRWA's activities as they relate to section 301(c) and other due diligence measures. For example, with the encouragement and funding of the USG, UNRWA has developed the successful Operations Support Officer (OSO) program in the West Bank and Gaza. As the GAO report notes, in April 2009, the Department approved funds for the establishment of an OSO program in Lebanon.

The GAO report includes several new policies undertaken by the Department to improve oversight by enhancing communication with UNRWA on issues related to 301(c). These procedures were designed to formalize already existing but less formal means of communication between the Department of State and UNRWA. In a similar vein, the Department will work with UNRWA to develop a formalized checklist of criteria including those mechanisms already used informally to evaluate UNRWA's conformance with the condition required by 301(c), such as the number of OSO inspections and checks against the UN Security Council Resolution 1267 list (Al Qaida and Taliban) sanctions regime. The Department will work together with UNRWA to develop criteria, as appropriate, as well as reporting requirements, the modalities of which will be included in future Frameworks for Cooperation beginning in 2010.

Screening Names of UNRWA contractors against Lists of Individuals and Entities of Concern to the United States

The Department of State is actively assessing the feasibility of this recommendation. State/PRM is in the process of discussing this issue with other personnel within the Department, from other U.S. Government agencies, and with UNRWA. UNRWA has confirmed that it already screens its list of potential vendors against the list of persons designated under UN Security Council Resolution 1267. UNRWA has also confirmed to the Department that it would use

3

information provided by us regarding potential individuals and entities of concern as a trigger to conduct its own investigations as relevant. (As the GAO report notes, in 2006 the UN declined a request from the Department to screen all of its potential contractual and financial arrangements against the list of specially designated nationals maintained by the Treasury Department's Office of Foreign Assets Control.)

The Department has some concerns that the resources required to undertake effective screening may not be commensurate with the benefits that would be achieved from such a program, in light of the costs that would likely be associated with screening and the controls that UNRWA already has in place. However, State/PRM, in coordination with other offices within the Department as well as other USG agencies, is actively reviewing and researching this matter to see whether there is a feasible mechanism to implement this recommendation.

Monitoring UNRWA' Commitments regarding Future Internal Audits

The Department of State concurs with this recommendation and notes that in January 2009, UNRWA committed in writing to conduct internal audits of key elements of UNRWA processes, including those related to appropriate inclusion of anti-terrorism clauses in UNRWA contracts as well as cash assistance. The Department believes that internal audits on these topics, as recommended by GAO, would prove beneficial to UNRWA's operations and continued conformance of the condition required by section 301(c). The Department understands that conducting these internal audits would result in additional costs to UNRWA, which already suffers from chronic underfunding. The Department is exploring funding options to enhance UNRWA's capacity for internal audits, including in these two areas.

APPENDIX VI: COMMENTS FROM THE UNITED NATIONS RELIEF AND WORKS AGENCY FOR PALESTINE REFUGEES IN THE NEAR EAST

unrwa
60 years

united nations relief and works agency for palestine refugees in the near east

unrwa headquarters gaza
office of the commissioner-general
c/o hq amman
p.o. box 140157
amman 11814
jordan

t +972 8 6777700
+962 6 5808556
f +972 8 6777699
+962 6 5808179

www.unrwa.org

7 May 2009

Dear Mr. Melito,

Thank you for requesting our comments on the draft GAO report, "Foreign Assistance: Measures to Prevent Inadvertent Payments to Terrorists under Palestinian Aid Programs Have Been Strengthened, but Some Weaknesses Remain" (GAO-PUB No. 09-622, GAO Code 320618).

UNRWA welcomes GAO's review, report and findings. The Agency cooperated fully with the review and appreciates GAO's collaborative and constructive approach throughout the process.

UNRWA will work closely with the US Department of State to further develop criteria to evaluate those internal processes and mechanisms that strengthen its compliance with US conditions of funding. UNRWA has also made a commitment that future internal UNRWA audits would assess the Agency's compliance with its neutrality/anti-terrorism policies for contractors as well as internal controls for cash assistance and will facilitate monitoring by State of this commitment.

I take this opportunity to confirm that UNRWA is committed, in accordance with UN principles and policies, to UN neutrality, transparency, accountability and conformance with donor funding conditions. I would also like to express my sincere appreciation for the vital support of the Government of the United States for the humanitarian and human development mission of the Agency.

Yours sincerely,

Karen Koning AbuZayd
Commissioner-General

Mr. Thomas Melito
Director, International Affairs and Trade
US Government Accountability Office
Washington DC
USA

APPENDIX VII: STAFF ACKNOWLEDGMENTS

Cheryl Goodman, Assistant Director; Ashley Alley; Debbie Chung; John Craig; Martin de Alteriis, Justin Fisher, Mitchell Karpman, Justin Monroe, Mary Moutsos; John Reilly; Suneeti Shah; Elizabeth Singer; and Omar Torres made key contributions to this report.

End Notes

[1] Throughout this report, we use the term "prime awardee" to refer to an organization that directly receives USAID contracts, grants, or cooperative agreements to implement U.S. assistance projects. "Subawardee" refers to an organization that receives subcontracts or subgrants from prime awardees for work on U.S. assistance projects.

[2] Consolidated Appropriations Act of 2008, Pub.Law No. 110-161, Dec. 26, 2007.

[3] This report addresses the extent to which USAID has applied its policies and procedures to new awards funded through the Economic Support Fund in the West Bank and Gaza Program for fiscal year 2008. A separate GAO review will address additional issues regarding the treatment, handling, and uses of all funds for the bilateral West Bank and Gaza Program in fiscal year 2008.

[4] *State, Foreign Operations, and Related Program Appropriations Bill.* 110th Cong., 1st sess. (June 18, 2007).

[5] See GAO, *Department of State (State) and United Nations Relief and Works Agency (UNRWA) Actions to Implement Section 301(c) of the Foreign Assistance Act of 1961,* GAO-04-276R (Washington, D.C.: Nov. 17, 2003).

[6] See GAO, *Foreign Assistance: Recent Improvements Made, but USAID Should Do More to Help Ensure Aid Is Not Provided for Terrorist Activities in West Bank and Gaza,* GAO-06-1062R (Washington, D.C.: Sept. 29, 2006).

[7] Section 657(c)(1), Consolidated Appropriations Act of 2008, PL 110-161, Dec. 26, 2007.

[8] Mission Order 21 cites several legal authorities for its antiterrorism procedures. These include (1) Executive Order 13224 (Sept. 23, 2001), which blocks property and prohibits transactions with persons who commit, threaten to commit, or support terrorism; (2) sections 2339A and 2339B of Title 18 of the U.S. Code which prohibit the provision of material support or resources for terrorist acts or to designated foreign terrorist organizations; and (3) Executive Orders 12947 (Jan. 23, 1995) and 13099 (Aug. 20, 1998) which prohibit transactions with terrorists who threaten to disrupt the Middle East peace process. Mission Order 21 also includes provisions of special relevance to the USAID Mission in the West Bank and Gaza in Section 559 of the Foreign Operations Export Financing and Related Programs Appropriations Act, 2006 (Pub. Law No. 109-102). Similar provisions have appeared in subsequent appropriations acts, including the Consolidated Appropriations Act of 2008.

[9] The list of individuals and entities subject to economic and trade sanctions based on U.S. foreign policy and national security goals is formally called the Specially Designated Nationals and Blocked Persons list and commonly referred to as the OFAC list. OFAC publishes the list as part of its efforts to administer and enforce U.S. sanctions programs.

[10] The UN Security Council's "Consolidated List established and maintained by the 1267 Committee with respect to Al-Qaida, Usama bin Laden, and the Taliban and other individuals, groups, undertakings and entities associated with them" is referred to as the UN 1267 list. The Security Council's Al-Qaida and Taliban Sanctions Committee established the list pursuant to paragraph 6 of Security Council resolution 1267 (Oct. 15, 1999) and the committee oversees governments' implementation of the three sanctions measures (assets freeze, travel ban, and arms embargo) imposed by the Security Council on individuals and entities on the list.

[11] 22 U.S.C. § 2221(c).

[12] GAO-06-1062R. These other types of assistance instruments include consulting agreements, letters of understanding, memorandums of understanding, and purchase orders.

[13] Since 2003, annual appropriation acts have required the Administrator of USAID to ensure that audits of all contractors and grantees, and significant subcontractors and subgrantees, under the West Bank and Gaza Program, are conducted on at least an annual basis. In furtherance of this requirement, the USAID Inspector General has implemented a program to audit these entities annually. USAID's Regional Inspector General must, according to its own policies, audit the prime awardees and significant subawardees every fiscal year. While a single awardee may receive multiple prime awards for services, only one of those prime awards is audited each fiscal year. The Regional Inspector General has defined significant subawards as those that have a cumulative cost of $300,000 or higher per fiscal year.

[14] The three prime awardees required to submit antiterrorism certifications had signed the certifications prior to the date of the award, as required.

[15] USAID may approve assistance to such a facility only if it determines that the purpose and practical effect of such assistance will not be to provide recognition to such a person or group.

[16] These four new prime awards required vetting because they were awarded to non-U.S. organizations for amounts greater than $25,000.

[17] We evaluated a random sample of 144 subawards for compliance with applicable requirements from Mission Order 21. In selecting our random sample, we selected two random subsamples—one consisting of 49 U.S. organizations and individuals and another consisting of 95 non-U.S. organizations and individuals—because the vetting requirements are only applicable to non-U.S. organizations. Of the 95 non-U.S. organizations, 9 were exempt from the vetting requirements, 51 were subject to pre-award vetting because the amount of the award exceeded $25,000, and the remaining 35 were for amounts below the $25,000 vetting threshold.

[18] Our sample included 14 grants, six of which were made to nongovernmental organizations and thus were required to have an antiterrorism certification, according to Mission Order 21. The remaining eight grants were made to either individuals or governmental entities and thus did not require an antiterrorism certification.

[19] We conducted a probability sample of new subawards, stratified by either U.S. or non-U.S. subawardees. With a probability sample, each subaward in the population had a non-zero probability of being included, and that probability could be computed for any member. Each sample element selected was subsequently weighted in the analysis to account statistically for all the members of the population. The result of the sample can be projected to the population from which it was selected. Because our sample selection was based on random selections, it was only one of a large number of samples that might have been drawn. Since each sample could have provided different estimates, we express our confidence in the precision of our particular sample's result as a 95 percent confidence interval (e.g., plus or

minus 7 percentage points). This is the interval that would contain the actual population value for 95 percent of the samples we could have drawn. As a result, we are 95 percent confident that each of the confidence intervals included within this report will include the true values in the study population.

[20] USAID provided us 6 sets of annotated mandatory clauses for a total of 14 separate subawards.

[21] This estimate was weighted to reflect the fact that we selected 49 out of a total of 101 U.S. subawards and 95 out of a total of 2,519 non-U.S. subawards. See appendix I for more information on our methodology.

[22] The International Convention for the Suppression of the Financing of Terrorism defines an offense under the convention to include an offense within the scope of and as defined in any of the nine treaties listed in the annex to the convention, as well as any other act intended to cause death or serious bodily injury to a civilian or any other person not taking an active part in the hostilities in a situation of armed conflict, when the purpose of such act is to intimidate a population or compel a government or international organization to do or abstain from doing any act. International Convention for the Suppression of the Financing of Terrorism, U.N. Doc A/RES/54/109 (Dec. 9, 1999).

[23] State reported that continued U.S. funding for UNRWA is contingent upon State's conclusion that UNRWA continues to take the steps required to meet the conditions required by section 301(c). As part of State's formal financial approval processes, State's Office of the Legal Adviser closely reviews all spending plans, taking section 30 1(c) and other legal requirements into consideration; these spending plans are cleared by all relevant bureaus with interests in the funding, with final approval by the Director of Foreign Assistance. Each contribution to UNRWA is approved by the Assistant Secretary of State's Bureau of Population, Refugees and Migration (PRM) based on a written paper that includes a section reviewing UNRWA's conformance with the condition required by section 301(c). However, we found that this written paper is not an evaluation or determination of UNRWA's conformance with conditions in section 301(c).

[24] GAO-04-276R.

[25] GAO-04-276R.

[26] In responding to a U.S. request that UN agencies vet prospective and current arrangements against the OFAC list, the UN Legal Counsel told State in a January 2006 letter that it would not be appropriate for the UN to establish a verification regime that uses a list developed by one member state, such as the OFAC list.

[27] UNRWA provided us with a list of roughly 20,000 contractors it paid between 2002 and 2009. We narrowed the list to about 15,000 contractors by, among other things, eliminating any record that only contained 1 part of an individual's name. We used a relatively basic methodology to identify potential matches. We did not find any perfect matches, since a perfect match between the two lists would require the records in each list to be identically matched, and we found that names in the two lists varied in the number of name parts, the translation of Arabic names to English, spelling, and the type of demographic information included. An example of a possible match would be when we found names in both lists that were similar but were spelled differently. Determining with greater confidence whether other names are a likely match requires additional research and more advanced procedures. See appendix I for more information on our methodology.

[28] UNRWA reported that it plans to submit additional information to State on any denials of requests for assistance arising from the Israeli "Operation Cast Lead" in the Gaza Strip from December 27, 2008 to January 19, 2009, in its semiannual compliance report covering the period from January 2009 to June 2009.

[29] UNRWA officials told us that following media reports alleging that people elected in March 2009 to positions in an UNRWA teachers' union were affiliated with political parties, the agency opened an investigation as required by and in accordance with UNRWA's Staff Rules and Regulations. That investigation is ongoing. UNRWA officials said disciplinary action will be taken if the results of the investigation show involvement of staff members in political activities contrary to UNRWA staff rules and regulations.

[30] The Commissioner-General launched a comprehensive organizational development initiative in late 2005 designed to strengthen and sustain UNRWA's capacity for program management and delivery, which resulted in an organizational development strategic plan for the 2006 to 2009 time period. Goals of the plan include ensuring UNRWA programs for refugees are more strategic and focused and an agency culture of accountability.

[31] GAO-04-276R.

[32] Under a UN policy, UNRWA officials said they do not screen contractors against donor country lists.

[33] UNRWA also reported that, in accordance with UN policy, it uses the UN Suspended/Removed Vendor Report, which identifies those vendors confirmed to be doing business in an unethical or corrupt manner, to screen contractors.

[34] We did not independently review the results of UNRWA's Department of Internal Oversight Services' internal audits because, under a current UNRWA policy, donor governments and respective agencies do not have access to the results of internal agency audits.

[35] The Special Hardship Assistance Program is an UNRWA Relief and Social Services program, which is comprised of food assistance and a cash subsidy for food of up to $40 per year per family member. This program is intended to provide a cushion of support to refugees in distress who are unable to earn a living because of a particularly difficult family situation, ensure minimum standards of nutrition and shelter, and intervene with cash grants in case of exceptional family difficulties.

[36] Under the UN Financial Regulations and Rules, the General Assembly appoints a Board of Auditors to perform the audit of the accounts of the UN and its funds and programs. The board is independent and solely responsible for the conduct of the audit, and it audits UNRWA's financial statements every 2 years. This board consists of three members, each of whom shall be the Auditor-General (or officer holding the equivalent title) of a member state.

End Nots for Appendix I

[1] GAO, *Department of State (State) and United Nations Relief and Works Agency (UNRWA) Actions to Implement Section 301(c) of the Foreign Assistance Act of 1961*, GAO-04-276R (Washington, D.C.: Nov. 17, 2003).

End Nots for Appendix III

[1] State said it does not currently limit its contributions to UNRWA's General Fund to specific purposes, but all U.S. contributions to UNRWA's Emergency Appeal for West Bank and Gaza are limited so that no U.S. funds are to be used for UNRWA's emergency cash assistance activities in West Bank and Gaza.

[2] The UN Administrative Tribunal Statute and Rules established the tribunal to hear and pass judgment on applications alleging non-observance of a staff member's contract or terms of appointment. An application is receivable before the UN Administrative Tribunal once the person concerned has taken the case to a joint appeals body that has communicated its opinion to the Secretary-General or in a case where the Secretary- General and the staff member concerned agree to submit applications directly to the tribunal.

INDEX

C

D

E

F

G

H

I

J

L

M

N

O

P

T